P9-DUN-242

GLIMPSES

GLIMPSES

THROUGH HOLOCAUST AND LIBERATION

BENJAMIN BENDER

North Atlantic Books
Berkeley, California

Published by
North Atlantic Books
P.O. Box 12327
Berkeley, California 94712

© 1995 Benjamin Bender
All Rights Reserved. Printed in the United States of America·

Cover and book design by Legacy Media, Inc.
Photos courtesy Benjamin and Sara Bender, except page 240, © Simon Chaput

Glimpses is sponsored by the Society for the Study of Native Arts and
Sciences, a nonprofit educational organization whose goals are to develop an
ecological and crosscultural perspective linking various scientific, social, and
artistic fields; to nurture a holistic view of arts, sciences, humanities, and
healing; and to publish and distribute literature on the relationship of mind,
body, and nature.

Library of Congress Cataloging-in-Publication Data
Bender, Benjamin, 1928–
    Glimpses : through Holocaust and liberation/Benjamin Bender.
        p. cm.
    ISBN 1-55643-209-7 (cloth).—ISBN 1-55643-208-9 (paper)
    1. Jews—Poland—Czestochowa—Persecutions.   2. Holocaust, Jewish
(1939-1945)—Poland—Czestochowa—Personal narratives.   3. Bender,
Benjamin, 1928– .   4. Buchenwald (Germany: Concentration camp).   5.
Holocaust survivors—Israel—Biography.   6. Czestochowa (Poland)—Ethnic
relations.   I. Title.
DS135.P62C86497 1995
940.53'18'092—dc20
[B]   95-4449
                                                                               CIP

1   2   3   4   5   6   7   8   9 / 99   98   97   96   95

DEDICATION

TO THE MEMORY of Ajzik and Blima Bender, my parents, Berek
Bender, my brother, Alter Malachowski, my wife's father, and
her sisters Busia, Breina, and Rachel, all lost in the Holocaust.
And to the memory of the righteous gentiles who inter-
vened to save my life and my wife's life: the unknown Polish
doctor in Buchenwald who chose to help me; Hatzia, the Pole
who helped many escaping the Baranowicze ghetto to join the
partisans; and Jan Grabowski, the Polish *Volksdeutscher* who let
my wife, her mother, aunt and cousin escape.

If you save a life, you save the whole world…

CONTENTS

1
—

PROLOGUE

IT'S INCONCEIVABLE half a century after liberation to search the vaults of memory for the unfinished stories and those that never began. The faces and the surroundings of the past are growing blurred, swept away by the winds of time. Many questions remain unanswered.

The shadow of the Holocaust still colors my life. The Germans are still on my mind. They took everything from me, even my tears. Fear is still planted in my heart: I abhor uniforms, emblems, marching soldiers, German shepherds. The months I spent in Buchenwald brought me to the threshold of extinction and changed my whole life. There was a song there sung by the inmates in the big camp when they marched, and it still lingers in my mind: *Buchenwald, Buchenwald, ich kann Dich nicht vergessen, weil Du mein Schicksal bist* (Buchenwald, Buchenwald, I cannot forget you, because you are my fate).

I don't write for a living; I just lived through the Holocaust, and like all survivors, I have a unique story to tell. I wrote this in English, my fourth language. Everything that follows is true—I saw these things with my own eyes or learned about them from witnesses. My wife Sara's story appears in parallel chapters and is faithful to her experiences and memories. This is not a history or an autobiography—just glimpses from the past…

A BOY OF CZESTOCHOWA

CZESTOCHOWA, POLAND. The name is self explanatory, it has a definite meaning: *czesto-sie-chowa* (it hides often). The town was surrounded by rolling hills and even the air had a special fragrance.

A train approaching the town would wriggle between the hills like a snake covetously swallowing the distance. Every day trains loaded with coal passed beneath the short overpass at Alley Boulevard. Skillful coal thieves would jump from the elevated overpass onto the speeding train, almost like in a movie, grab lumps of coal, throw them on the ground, then jump expertly down to collect them.

Shortly before the outbreak of World War II, the *Schnellzug* (torpedo train) had been introduced, and would pass with a frightful roar to the delight of the children. As the train approached the town, the spire of the monastery on the sacred Jasna Gora (bright mountain) would appear and disappear, shielded by the hills and luscious greenery.

September is always special in Poland because of the golden Polish autumn, glorified by poets and writers. But the September of 1939 was different, sadly heralding the end of a dream. The pale sun was still warm, but the shadows got deeper, darker. The rustic leaves covered the ground in a rich display of fiery colors, gleaming frivolously in the sunset. The crushed leaves had a fragrance, promising the beginning of a new cycle of life. Public parks in autumn were deserted, benches desolate, no traces of yesterday. On those benches love had been declared, promises made, friendships born.

A school year begins in September. I had a bright blue school emblem on my navy blue uniform sleeve, trimmed with silver threads, a number in the center. I was eleven, proud of my navy blue hat with its short visor and torch emblem. My new uniform, custom made, had silver buttons. The coat was long, similar to those worn by Polish officers. My school book had a catechism on the first page: *Per aspera ad astra* (through suffering to stars). It wasn't exactly like that.

The schoolyard was paved with gravel, the window frames of Axer's Gymnasium were blue. This private school was located on Ferdinand Foch Street. (The Poles had a liking for French and Italian war heroes.) At the entrance was a huge seductive orchard whose succulent fruits tasted even better than those served by my mother. In the Axer's orchard I played Tarzan with Aviv Rosyner. Aviv Rosyner was heavyset, bespectacled, with small eyes, and bubbles of saliva in the corners of his mouth. His name, Aviv, was unusual, because *aviv* in Hebrew means spring. (He never would get to enjoy the spring of his life, though, despite his name.) Aviv liked to be a leader. During one of these games, Aviv, hidden among the branches on top of a tree, jumped on me unexpectedly. The weight of his body knocked me to the ground. He broke my elbow, which was in a cast for many weeks. Because of the oath of friendship my parents never knew who did it.

Where was the beginning? The old house of Fajglowicz,

Blima Szylit Bender, Benjamin's mother,
in Czestochowa, Poland, c.1925.

Wielunska Street 4. Up the street, very near, was the monastery of Jasna Gora, a historical shrine. Down the street was the marketplace where on Tuesdays horses, cows, pigs, geese, chickens were sold. To ascertain the age of a horse the Polish peasants would look curiously into its mouth. I wondered if the horse's age was ever proven, but for sure an occasional peasant lost a finger!

My grandparents, the Szylits, had a small leather store. The size of the store and the volume of business seemed unlikely to support a single person, but it supported nine at a time. I could never understand the secret of Meyer Szylit's success. The store was full of smelly hides that they bought from a local tannery. Srulek, Meyer's son, cut the hard hides with a curved knife. The peasants, in order to buy a leather sole, or soles, would hand him a paper cutout which was a replica of the requested sole. Srulek's cut was professional. The curved knife would glide smoothly at a slanted angle along the line marked with a pencil.

Meyer had another son, Schmul, and five daughters, Blima, Mania, Fela, Sara, Anna. During World War I, Schmul served in the Austro-Hungarian army. After the war ended he didn't return to Poland, but settled and married in Germany. He was living in Ludwigsburg, near Stuttgart. Just before the outbreak of World War II, Mania left Czestochowa for Sosnowiec. She resisted the pressure of her parents to marry an old rich man. She preferred a man her own age, a handsome and articulate fellow named Olszewski. They had a coffee shop. During the war, Sara married a poor tailor. Not being able to find an apartment, they were forced to live with their parents. Anna never married. Srulek married shortly before the war.

Blima married Ajzik Bender, a handsome bon vivant who was an administrator. These were my parents. My father managed the property of some affluent Polish landlords who lived in Zakopane and Krynica, and some who were living abroad, even on the French Riviera.

Czestochowa had two main markets. The *stary rynek* (old market), was a place of the Jewish merchants. The deals were consummated quickly, with a firm hand shake, no signatures required, a man's word was a man's honor. The market swarmed with beggars, some demented ones, strolling aimlessly, talking and gesticulating to themselves, carrying burlap bags on their backs—homeless. The beggars scared the children, especially the fearful dwarf woman, stocky, bowlegged, with her small, but oversize features. She was always petrified, running back and forth, disappearing with a whimper. Everyone in town called her Rywele.

Along Alley Boulevard, stretching from the old market to the Jasna Gora monastery was the commercial center of Czestochowa. On the weekends the well-to-do would stroll aimlessly, dressed in their best. The display was to show the measure of their wealth to their friends and neighbors. On both sides of the street there were many stores: Szelcer's dress shop, the Bata shoe store, Plutos candy and chocolate, the Stylowy and Luna cinemas. Further up was the Europa night club where a jazz band played in the evenings at the corner of Slaska Street. To the right of the Stawski dress shop there was a jewelry store where I would window shop, marveling at the Swiss watches. Close to the Eden cinema was the elegant Ziemianska, known for delicious pastry.

The Poles had a market of their own, in the vicinity of Jasna Gora. Not far from the market were two adjacent streets, St. Barbara and St. Roch. Saints didn't live there. Punks wielding knifes were a vital part of that street landscape. A cop was a rarity, always in demand, but never seen. The cops were called *glina* by the punks, which means clay.

Far out at the extreme right of the market was a seltzer factory owned by the Zuckermans, known for their delicious and refreshing drinks on hot summer days, especially the *Lesna woda* (forest drink). The cold drink was bubbly and invigorating.

Next to St. Roch Street was a church. Andrzej, a retarded boy, fifteen years old, with a hunchback, would swing a giant church bell. To set the bell in motion he had to pull a heavy rope, swinging and dangling in the air grotesquely. The worshippers stood patiently in line to touch his hunchback which was supposed to bring good luck. My grandfather admonished me to stay away from the church, promising harsh heavenly punishment in the event I didn't heed his warning (which I didn't because of my curiosity).

Up Wielunska Street, the sacred Jasna Gora. The old monastery had the Byzantine tapestry of the *Matka Boska* (the Black Madonna), known for heavenly miracles. In the sixteenth century the Primate Kordecki successfully repulsed the armies of King Gustav of Sweden after a long siege. The cannonballs used by the attackers are still cemented inside the walls of the monastery. It is said that the Black Madonna had tears in her eyes when a Cossack cavalryman cut her face with his sword. Every year, in swarming processions, walking hundreds of miles, their feet bleeding, believers were infatuated with the sight of the sacred place. They came in droves, in pursuit of blessings and cures. Not once did they collapse from thirst or fatigue. Surprisingly, for unknown reasons, they drank pickle water to revitalize themselves. To find accommodations for thousands wasn't easy. They slept in barns, stables, or under the starry summer sky.

During winter, when the white puffy snow covered the hills of Jasna Gora, I would take my sleigh out of the cellar. I had a friend who drove the sleigh expertly, Kuba Rosensaft, seventeen, a daring driver. Going downhill had its scary moments. The sleigh would speed wildly, the cold wind ringing in our ears, our cheeks red, noses nippy, ears needle-like, breath steaming like a boiling tea kettle. The hardest part was to walk uphill carrying the sleigh for another ride.

From Wielunska Street 4, my family moved to Kopernika

20, near the new post office building. In my eyes it was like moving from a village to a metropolis. The property belonged to the Bolkowskas and consisted of two houses facing each other, with a huge yard in between. Further down from Kopernika Street towards Wolnosci Street was the Szpalten house. Days before the outbreak of World War II, Szpalten, sensing the tax office on his heels, escaped to Palestine, leaving his family behind.

On the corner of Kopernika Street and the left corner of Wolnosci Street was the infamous *Endeks* building of the Polish fascists, the Jew baiters, who forbid Polish peasants to enter Jewish stores, painting signs on the store windows *Nie kupuj u Zyda* (don't patronize a Jew). The *Endeks* were the worst, seething with hatred and ignorance.

My mother had so-called Aryan features. She was a dark blond, with blue eyes, able to pass the skillful Polish race scrutiny undetected. One time, around Christmas 1938, while shopping, she witnessed a drunken Polish soldier attack an old Jew with an empty vodka bottle for no apparent reason. Curious passersby stood around watching the scene with total indifference to the possible maiming or murder of an old man. His face was bleeding, blood on his silver beard. His hat was on the snowy ground. In vain he tried to cover his face. Without hesitation my mother pushed her way through the crowd, positioning herself between the soldier and the Jew.

"Why are you attacking this old defenseless man?" she demanded.

The soldier, unsteady, swaying back and forth, mumbled, "He is a dirty old Jew, I hate him," then he added, "A Polish lady like you shouldn't defend this damned old bastard. Look around you, nobody cares."

Then my mother, with all her force, punched him in the face. The soldier collapsed like a chopped down tree. The crowd began to disperse without any comment. Some were very unhappy. The old man, scared to death, picked up his trampled hat and uttered some words of deep appreciation. He was unaware that she was Jewish.

"*Dziekuje Pani serdecznie* (Lady, thank you from my heart)." He began to walk briskly, looking back fearfully. The soldier was prostrate on the ground, motionless, probably in a deep slumber.

The next day the local newspaper reported that a brave Polish woman heroically defended an old Jew who was being attacked by a drunken soldier, a shameful event staining the Polish honor. The reporter underlined that moral values and bravery are an integral part of the Polish heritage. The reporter concluded, "I would be happy to shake the hand of this brave Polish patriot."

On the other corner of Kopernika Street, adjacent to Slaska Street, was the new modern post office, the pride of the town, with revolving doors, not well known in those waning days of 1939. I used those revolving doors with my brother ad nauseam. Opposite the post office building was a Gothic church, with spires shooting into the skies. Weeks before the war the place was seething with German spies, diligently preparing the ground for the German invasion.

The house at Kopernika 20 had a high wooden green fence. The entrance was shoddy, paint peeling off, a gate without a handle. Up on the right side there was a rusty pull chain to activate the bell. In the daytime children used the bell indiscriminately, and during the night so did the drunkards, searching in vain for the right address.

Piotr was the janitor, tall, lanky, with a protruding Adam's apple, impoverished, with many children. On Saturdays he used to light up fires in the Jewish stoves for meager pay and a piece of *challah* (soft braided bread). Piotr's children were always soiled, snot under their noses.

The huge backyard was a wonderful playground, devouring my inexhaustible energies. The recurrent requests from our maid Marysia to come up for supper were unheeded. Adjacent to the backyard was a sprawling wild orchard, in the center of which was a meadow, the soccer field. I played soccer with the *Skutzim* (young *goyim*—gentiles). On many occasions we used a ragball, a leather soccer ball being beyond reach. The soccer games went on until the late evening hours, regardless even of pouring rain. The ball, soaked with water, would be heavy, hurting our feet, but enhancing the delight of sportsmanship.

I had a friend, not really a close friend, but we used to play ragball. His name was Wowek and he was blond, with wavy hair and blue eyes. His father, Moshe Wien, was a poor tailor who struggled all his life to make a living. Occasionally I would watch him work. He used a black press iron filled with burning coals that emitted a fine cloud of moisture permeated with a smell of burning material. The slacks or suits he ironed were covered with a yellowish piece of linen, burned and tattered.

Wowek was a drop-out but he had a rare spark of ingenuity. The orchard was never tended and the fruit, apples and pears, never ripe. Wowek would carry a large straw basket during autumn days, and would pick the small pears from the trees. He carried this heavy load to his attic, storing the pears in heaps of straw.

Once, during a snow storm, Wowek invited me up to the

attic to share some of the pears. *No* one in winter could offer such succulent fruit! We sat together, sinking in the heap of straw, having the time of our lives.

During the hot summer, the orchard was a place for street gamblers and prostitutes. The street gamblers played blackjack. Sitting on the ground, they kept their money in their hats. The money was never counted during the game, a bad omen for the players. The gamblers liked the children watching the game curiously. Each of the gamblers wanted a child to stand next to him for good luck. The gamblers were generous, the winners and the losers as well. Money treats were common and anxiously expected.

When night descended, the orchard swarmed with prostitutes entertaining their customers. At daylight, condoms were littered all over the orchard. Children, unaware of these "night escapades," would use the condoms as balloons, to the abhorrence of the adults who were at loss as to how to dissuade them from doing so.

Adjacent to the orchard was Washington Street. At that time I wasn't aware who Washington was. Along the narrow street, the hackney coaches (*droshky*), would wait for customers just across from the Landau doll factory. During the winter, the *droshky* coachmen wore long coats, and would stomp their feet and blow into their palms. The snow, crisp, pure white, would screech like broken glass under foot. The coachmen were equipped with miniature bottles of vodka, *szczeniaczek*. Their bushy mustaches were covered with icicles, firm like wires. The empty bottles were collected by children for the store refund.

During the summer days, I would go with Lucek Rosenman to the Warta river. The weeping willows, in silent embrace, were touching the rapid stream. We would chase butterflies, trying in vain to catch them. We searched diligently for flat stones, and would throw them in a horizontal motion on the surface of the flowing river. Occasionally the stones would jump off the surface like grass hoppers, leaving wide floating rings, then vanish in the river. Lucek Rosenman was a gregarious guy, punkish, aggressive, but a good friend. As I was chronically shy, Lucek didn't spare efforts to introduce me to girls, which he did with some success.

With the guidance of my father, I frequented two wellknown delis in Czestochowa: the Abramowitz, on Alley Boulevard, and the Grohman, located at the old market. Both were famous for their sausages, liverwurst, smoked goose, smoked turkey, and a rich variety of other tempting delicacies which I couldn't resist. I was enchanted by these frequent visits, and at night would dream of owning one of the delis.

Another peerless place was a pastry shop, on the corner of Wolnosci Street and Alley Boulevard. The napoleons were out of this world, as well as the chocolate mushrooms filled with yellow custard.

My childhood was imbued with secret desires and unfulfilled wishes. There were matters close to my heart: a bicycle, a scout knife, a sleigh, or a watch. I dreamed of having a watch. I was envious of my friends who had watches; having one was a taste of maturity and importance. I would stand for hours before the jewelry store window which was filled with Swiss watches, and I would fantasize owning an Omega or a Cyma watch.

One day a miracle happened. My brother Berek and I received two beautiful Kinsley brand watches with phosphorescent numerals. They had been sent from Germany by our uncle

Schmul. He could hardly afford to buy such expensive gifts but he had a good heart and he did it. Overjoyed, I walked everywhere with my left hand extended to show it off with pride. The next day I went to see *The Last of the Mohicans* at the Luna cinema. As I watched the movie tensely, I would occasionally look at the watch which was glowing in the darkness of the theater. Suddenly, I felt my throat burning. I couldn't swallow, the pain was overwhelming. I left the theater sick and my parents immediately called a doctor. The diagnosis was fearsome: I had diptheria and there was no medicine to treat it. Nothing could be done except praying and crying; my parents did both. With the high fever I was hallucinating. I saw my watch grow bigger and sprout hands and legs. It joined the watches in the jewelry store window and they were all dancing and leaping together in my mind. After a long struggle, I overcame the illness. The watch had been a precious talisman to me.

My father's parents, the Benders, lived at Garncarska Street 18. The street was ugly, the road paved with cobblestones (*kocie lby*—cat's heads). The street had a ghetto face even before the ghetto was established. Avraham Bender and Esther Bender had six children—three sons and three daughters. Avraham had a salt warehouse at Mostowa Street. He purchased salt wholesale at the Wieliczki salt mines and would resell to stores. My father Ajzik was the oldest, next was Schlomo, and Yehuda was the youngest. Schlomo had a deep pleasant voice and he often sang, accompanied by my father who would play mandolin. Yehuda wasn't the brightest among the others, but good natured, generous, always willing to help. He respected his father highly, yet, in July of 1939, less than two months before the outbreak of war, Yehuda departed as an *Halutz* (pioneer) for Palestine, against the will of his parents. Disregarding his parental guidance, he made a choice of his own.

The step Yehuda took at that time was considered rebellious and revolutionary. The apocalyptic war was coming, but no one wanted to believe. Neville Chamberlain, intoxicated with futile hopes, was victoriously waving a signed document, proclaiming to the world the dawn of peace "in our times." The dreams would soon be shattered. Adolf Hitler was screaming hysterically on the radio, but his threats remained unheeded. He was considered a maniac, to be left alone.

My parents sensed the gathering storm, and beset by agonizing despair, they approached the Primate of the monastery of Jasna Gora with a request to save the lives of my brother and me. Like my mother, I had blond hair and blue eyes, and perhaps could qualify to join the ranks of the choir boys. We were there with my parents when the meeting took place. The answer was a flat no. The well-being of the monastery couldn't be endangered because of two Jewish boys; the repercussions could be severe. Our fate was sealed.

At the end of August 1939, my father was called to arms, leaving abruptly, destination unknown, a Jew to serve the cause of antisemitic Poland. (During the Polish independence war of 1920 he had served under Marshal Pilsudzki who defeated the Russian calvary in a battle known as *Cud nad Wisla*— "Miracle on the Vistula River.") The family bicycle was taken away by the Polish military to be used to fight the superb, modern, mechanized, invading Nazi forces.

On September 1, 1939, German motorized units, with the support of Stukas (Messerschmidt fighter planes), smashed through the Polish defenses, shattering the myth of traditional Polish bravery. The Polish army, under the dull Marshal Rydz-Smigly, based on obsolete, outmoded warfare, couldn't stop the German blitz. The fearless, mounted lancers of Duke Sapiecha charged the German tanks like a wooden cavalry with pointed spears. The German armor mowed them down mercilessly. In a matter of weeks, Warsaw lay in ruins, razed by Stukas. The Teutonic rage was a warning for England and France to soon enter the arena of war.

Poland was dying in dignity. The indiscriminate bombing of civilians was the first, but not the last. The display of barbarity shook the conscience of the world. The Polish sailors of Westerplatte put up a gallant stand, but it was short-lived. Even the German high command paid them a hero's tribute. The defeat of Poland in 1939 ended her tragic and unfulfilled drive for independence.

Jews had first arrived in Czestochowa in 1765; by the beginning of World War II there were over thirty-five thousand living in the city. There were three Jewish schools and the community played an important role in industry and commerce. It all ended in a day. On September 1, 1939, German forces entered town and the very next day a reign of terror was set in motion against the Jewish intelligentsia—doctors, lawyers, businessmen. About 800 people were chosen for prompt executions or deportation to Buchenwald and Dachau. The Germans were guided by Polish informers who performed their jobs quickly and efficiently. They never entered the monastery…they had no reason.

A GIRL OF BARANOWICZE

BARANOWICZE IS in the eastern part of Poland, at a main railroad junction. Freight trains loaded with coal, timber, iron, and fuel heading as far as Gdansk would pass through day and night, roaring.

The town was a happy town, vibrant, imbued with Jewish culture and tradition. The strong currents of Jewish nationalism were reflected in many organizations like Hashomer Hatzair, Gordonia, Bethar and others aspiring for a homeland. A lot of young people in the 1920s and 1930s, against the wishes of their parents, left Baranowicze to go to Palestine, to work the fields as pioneers.

At this time the Jews of Baranowicze numbered about twelve thousand. The population fluctuated with the influx of Jews from other parts of Poland. Baranowicze was dispersed in a wide radius, consisting of a new and old city. The Jews lived in both parts of town, some mingling with the Polish population, but most distancing themselves from Polish culture and tradition. There were many private Jewish schools, teaching Hebrew, Jewish culture, Polish and all other elementary subjects as well. There were also many churches, synagogues, and one impressive Orthodox *Cerkwa* (church) at the corner of Grafska, Pilsudzkiego, and Orla. Jewish commerce was flourishing, with stores, small businesses, shoemakers, tailors, glaziers, blacksmiths, a tannery, and a mill. In the new part of the town were numerous stores selling imported fabrics and domestic made, for suits and dresses. There was also a Plutos candy store, bakeries, ice cream parlors, and a Pan cinema. Goods from all corners of Poland were available. The marketplace hummed with life on business days. Peasants from nearby villages and hamlets would converge with their produce. From the stands they sold eggs, chickens, geese, vegetables, butter and sour cream from huge clay jugs, even huge loaves of home made bread.

On Jewish holidays the well-to-do Jews would stroll the main streets to show off their newly acquired dresses and suits. Everybody scrutinized each other to evaluate how expensive the dresses and the suits might be. This habit of display was an integral part of everyday life. Mothers looked at the well-dressed children, wondering aloud who the successful dressmaker was. Jews, not all of them, were enjoying a good life, making money in business supplying the needs of the local population. With the advent of summer and the vacation time for the children, the well-to-do would rush to the resorts with hopes of gaining some weight. This attitude was well implanted in the Jewish tradition: a round belly was synonymous with a rich merchant; a flat stomach was a certificate of poverty or a lower place in society.

Nevertheless the rich helped the very poor with food and meals. The poor Jewish students studying in the *yeshivot* to be certified Rabbis were supported by many of the well-to-do families. It was considered a sacred act to render such support. Many of the great *Zaddikim* ("just ones"—sages) came from eastern Poland.

—

ALTER MALACHOWSKI was a prosperous merchant in Baranow-icze. With his wife Celia (called Zivia) he operated a small general store selling groceries. Their oldest daughter was named Sara and there were three other daughters. (Another, older daughter, Pesha, died from meningitis, and an infant son died after his *brit*—circumcision.) Sara attended the Tarbut private school. She was learning Hebrew, which underlined her parents' desire to bring up their daughters in the finest Jewish tradition even while many Jews in other parts of Poland were acquiring Polish first names, trying to ride the uncomfortable waves of assimilation. (Many Jews in Poland proudly and happily acquired Polish names in their drive to assimilation. Names like Jerzy, Janek, Mietek, Jurek, Boleslaw, Tadek, Wacek, and Antek were chosen so as not to differentiate them in the hostile Polish environment. These futile efforts didn't procure a permit of acceptance.)

Sara was strong and fearless, a tomboy, mercilessly punching the *Skutzim* on many occasions. Her uncle, who emigrated before the war to Argentina, had given her the nickname Suslik; some more outspoken called her Zulik (a rascal). She had straight black hair cut short, with bangs on her forehead, and gleaming brown eyes. Sara was Alter's favorite daughter. She would ride with him on bicycles along the banks of the Myszanka river and into the nearby forest to collect mushrooms. From her father she learned to love nature, to listen to the silent language of whispering trees. Being a rascal, she was warned repeatedly by her father to be good. "If you don't behave yourself, I will marry you off to a rabbi with a long beard." ("Rabbi" at that time was synonymous with an old man.) Af-

The Malachowski family in Baranowicze 1936: Sara is seated on the right, Alter and Celia (Zivia), her parents, are in the center, and two of her sisters, Rachel and Breina, are at the left; behind her is her cousin Grunia.

ter these "threats" Sara would cry and say "I don't want an old rabbi."

Sara's parents had a spacious log house in the old part of the city with a large kitchen that was the center of life. There was a huge baker's oven made of white tiles in which Zivia would bake *challah* for Friday and Saturday. In the fall, wooden barrels would be brought in to make sauerkraut. In the backyard was an open fireplace, a primus with a bellows, where they would cook cranberries, strawberries, blackberries, blueberries, black currants, and cherries for jam and preserves in a big copper kettle. The big vats for the laundry would be set up there too, to boil everything every three months, and the whole backyard would be full of clothes hanging to dry (except in winter when the attic was used). It would take a week to iron everything and special workers came in to do it all. Help was always around to milk the goats and to chop the wood—

Nadzia the maid, and Kostus who tended the animals, both lived in the house. Life was simple, serene and undisturbed.

The backyard also had a well that served four families living in adjacent houses. Next door was the shoemaker, a poverty-stricken man with six sons who inherited the house and a back-breaking trade. Zivia would provide them with food for the traditional Sabbath meal. On the other side was a family of *Volksdeutsche*, Poles of German heritage, who would join the Malachowskis for holiday feasts. Across the street was a Russian Orthodox pope (*batuszuka*—priest) and his family.

Adjacent to the house was a neighbor's orchard, and Sara and her friends would climb the trees and pick the fruit, a game like hide and seek, played with boys. Soccer with a ragball was also popular. During summers they would play along the nearby railroad tracks and place long construction nails on the rails and wait for the trains to pass over them, producing sharp knives. They would walk along the river chasing butterflies and skipping stones across the water.

In the winter, when the ground was covered by snow, Alter would take the girls in a horse-drawn sleigh. They all wore fur coats and hats, and woolen gloves, and they covered their knees with bearskins. The steaming horse would pull the sleigh to the accompaniment of the ringing of little bells on his neck, and the girls would be quiet, cuddled together like little kittens. Kostus would take them to school with the sleigh every winter morning.

———

THE WINTER of 1939 was unusually cold. It was only November, the beginning. The frozen ground was covered with a thick blanket of snow, and the tree branches were full of imaginary shapes, collapsing under the weight of the snow, sending a hail of glittering sparks in the air.

Baranowicze was of strategic importance, being situated on a railroad line linking Germany from the west and Russia from the east. In September the Germans, in a surprise attack, had invaded Poland and World War II began. In a matter of weeks the demise of Poland was complete. The signing of the Protocol of Non-Aggression between von Ribentrop and Molotov once again brought the division of Poland, tempered by many divisions throughout her tragic history. Baranowicze came under Russian control.

After moving to the river Bug, the Russians took over a large swath of Polish territory, rich sprawling farm land known as the breadbasket of Poland. Life with the Russians wasn't easy. Merchants, store owners, were considered the enemies of communism. Many were arrested, some disappeared without a trace, their businesses confiscated, Sara's parents' included. The Russians took over some rooms of the Malachowski house and a young Russian, Yuri, was placed there to live.

The servants were let go and the girls helped with the chores. Alter rented a field to raise potatoes, carrots and cabbage, and the basement quickly filled with food. They still had their animals—goats, geese, ducks and chickens—and soon Sara's two grandmothers came to live in the house. There was no food in the markets, the stores were empty, and it was dangerous to have any valuables. Alter constructed a hidden storeroom with a double wall and filled it with bolts of fabric to sell on the black market. He did all kinds of work to make money now that the store was gone.

Little information was available about the rest of Poland under German occupation. Nobody believed the fantastic stories of ghettos and camps and human soap, and most were bitter under the harsh Russian control.

In less than two years the Russians were retreating from the advancing German forces. Yuri came to Alter and said, "Comrade, I have a big truck and I would like you to come with me to Russia, to run away."

"No, I cannot. I have a wife and four little girls, I can't leave them," Alter said.

"Bring them too! Come!"

"No...I cannot do that."

And so Yuri left for the east with the retreating Russians.

4

INTO THE GHETTO

On September 16, 1939 a *Judenrat* was established under Leon Kopinski to collaborate with the German authorities in Czestochowa, and an unarmed Jewish police was formed. On Christmas Day the great synagogue was set afire. We were still living at 20 Kopernika Street, a non-Jewish area. Because of my Aryan appearance I didn't even wear the armband with a star of David.

During my father's absence from home we had difficulty making ends meet. The money was scarce and was soon depleted. In order to survive, my mother tried with some success to make money on the black market. Then, in the spring of 1940, we rented out a room in our apartment.

Hanka Laufbahn had arrived in Czestochowa from Krakow. She was of medium height. Her hair was dark, her eyes brown. She was young looking, in her early thirties. Before the war she had taught Polish literature, Latin and philosophy. There were stacks of books in her room. She didn't work but she had the money to spend on expensive food like butter and ham, which was out of reach in those days.

I got very attached to her. I was eager to learn and she was ready to teach me. The numerous books in her room drew my attention. For the first time in my life I heard about Romain

Rolland, Thomas Mann, Stephan Zweig, Heinrich Heine and others.

In the evenings when the wind howled outside the house, she would recite poetry, unraveling the world of beauty. The room was warm, the fireplace crackling with flying sparks. I would lean my head on her shoulder, infatuated by her voice. She instructed me to read books and then we would discuss the writer. My world changed instantly. I learned Latin. The most complex problems turned out to be easy and accessible. She taught me how to write essays which I did with moderate success. Socrates, Solon, Demonstheses, Pythagoras, Aristotle, Archimedes came alive.

I was more than happy to shop for her, to carry her food basket. She was quite aware of the attention I paid to her. She didn't mind; on the contrary, she seemed pleased with my affection for her. On many occasions she mentioned her brother, a lawyer, who was living in French Madagascar and was trying to bring her over. I was afraid to lose her because she gave such a lift to my life. I lost interest in sports, in games, and waited for the moment when she would allow me to join her.

I was expanding my horizons thanks to her. With a touch of her magic wand she opened a small window to a closed world. She said to me more than once, "We are all part of this immense universe, like stars in a big constellation. The war will be over soon," she said. "This is a struggle between darkness and light. Sooner or later the light will have the upper hand."

On many occasions she invited me to join her for a walk. We used to go to a public park, sit on a bench, and marvel at the beauty of nature. Often I pondered the question of how she could find a common language with a boy half her age.

But I sensed a bond of spirit between us. She didn't have any friends. I was eager to learn, to understand the mechanics of the human mind, to understand why wrong is stronger than right. She didn't have all the answers and I had too many questions. As time went by I felt the distance between us narrowing. She was delighted by my interest in Latin and philosophy, and my progress in writing was good. We shared a knowledge of and love for Polish literature.

She couldn't understand how a nation which produced Goethe, Schiller, Schoppenhauer, Leibnitz, Beethoven, and Heinrich Heine could become this state of savages pretending to rule the world. She was optimistic, and claimed that the Germans wouldn't go too far. I didn't question her judgment.

Occasionally, though, she became despondent, locking her room. Not really curious, but worrying about her, I would stare through the crack of the door, my heart pounding like a hammer, fearful for her. She was crying, wiping away her tears. I realized that she was unhappy. Under a facade of smiles she was suffering, being all alone facing the unknown. I knew I couldn't be of any help. This was her life and I wasn't the one to be trusted with all her problems.

The months she stayed with us changed my life. I matured mentally, knowing what I wanted to be when the time of awakening arrived. I wanted to offer myself to noble ideas for the betterment of human conditions, to help people find their way in the maze of life.

Once during our discussions she said to me: "I am proud of you and I am thankful to you." I didn't ask questions, and probably blushed, stunned by her statement. Was this a two-way street? What could I offer her? Nothing.

When my father returned from the army, Hanka Laufbahn left our apartment. For weeks I was sick, despondent, I lost interest in everything. I coveted her presence, the softness of her voice, her warm smile, her compassion when I was at a loss to solve a problem. She had always been next to me, willing to help, to explain with patience.

My father had unexpectedly arrived home in the middle of 1940, scared to death. After the rout by the Germans, my father's defeated unit retreated towards Lwow. With the signing of the pact between Molotov and von Ribentropf, the Russians had moved their troops to the Bug river from the east. The Germans were deployed on the west bank. The remnants of the Polish army surrendered to the Russians in Lwow. The Russians set the Polish soldiers free.

My father then had an opportunity to apply for Russian citizenship and move deep into Russian territory to work in a coal mine at Dombas. He wasn't ready for that. His second choice was to cross the river San and get to the German side in order to return to Czestochowa, which is what he did.

The crossing of the river San was dangerous, arranged by well paid Polish smugglers. On the German side the Jews weren't allowed to use trains. By mistake he took the wrong train, one filled with high ranking Polish officers. The train was heading for Katyn (where about fifteen thousand Polish officers were later executed on the order of Stalin). He managed to change trains at the last moment.

For many weeks he remained at home, and then he got a job in a hospital for people stricken with typhus fever, a sickness caused by deadly bacteria, *Rickettsia Prowazecki*. The sickness was transferred by infected lice. He had an immunity; he had had typhus during the first World War. But very soon the hospital was liquidated by the Germans, the patients shot to death. A second carnage of Jewish people took place in August 1940, when about a thousand young men were sent to a labor camp in Cieszanow, where they perished.

Soon after, while walking alone on Washington Street, I was approached by two *Hitlerjugend* in paramilitary uniforms with long hunting knives in their holsters. A Polish "friend" of mine who stood nearby, started to scream and point at me, "*Zyd, Zyd!*" The two blocked my way, one on the right and the other on the left. I was in real trouble. In a flash I made a very dangerous decision. The one on the right was the strongest and he meant business. His hand was on the hilt of his knife. I surprised him with a quick blow to his nose and he rolled down on the sidewalk. I started to run. I was running for my life.

When I reached the house I could hardly breathe, overwhelmed by my reckless action. I told my mother the whole story. She was in tears. In a matter of minutes the house was surrounded by dozens of *Hitlerjugend*. Their intentions were clear: to search the building for me. I watched them through the crack of a window, my heart pounding.

Unexpectedly, a German priest from the gothic church not far from our house appeared outside. He knew our family, he knew me, too. After a heated discussion and much persuasion, he succeeded in dissuading them from their attempt to capture me and turn me over to the Gestapo. They didn't all leave, however, and some were on constant lookout near the house. I didn't leave the building for two weeks, finally slipping out after dark.

My family moved to the ghetto on April 9, 1941 and it was

sealed off on August 23. The ghetto consisted of ugly streets surrounded by barbed wire. The streets had probably come into existence in the eighteenth century when the first seventy-five Jewish residences were recorded in Czestochowa. Life in the ghetto was very depressing. Dilapidated houses, no pavement, cobblestone streets. The conditions were deplorable. Two families living in one small apartment. We were lucky to find a place to live.

The trauma of leaving Kopernika 20, overflowing with beautiful memories of my childhood, was devastating. When I entered the ghetto surrounded by barbed wire, the greenery disappeared, the landscape changed from brightness to darkness. Everything got narrow, small, ugly. The people I knew weren't the same. Germans watching the ghetto entrance gate, Jewish police trying to please the Germans.

The ghetto had no trees. It was located in the oldest part of the city. Jews had already been living there, small merchants, bakers, carpenters, tailors, and porters struggling to make a living. Before the war I never came to this part of the city except to visit my grandparents. But it was different then. They had a spacious apartment, and on Friday evenings when I would arrive with my brother, the table would be covered with a white tablecloth, brass candle holders and good food.

The Jews in the ghetto now acted strangely, walking nervously, looking back often, sensing unexpected danger. The barbed wired surrounding the ghetto was a sad reminder that our freedom ended at the fence. The Jewish police were aloof, and wore special uniforms. They collaborated with the Germans. On many occasions they even beat up Jews in the presence of the Germans.

Because of my Aryan appearance, I would often leave the ghetto to secure food. Once I almost paid with my life. I was coming back with a pail full of jam. A Polish youngster pointed at me, screaming "*Zyd!*" The German guard started to laugh, then I said to him calmly, in good German, "*Ich bin keine Jude, er ist ein Jude* (I am not a Jew, the other guy must be a Jew)." The German guard approached the Polish youngster, lowering his rifle. The Polish kid ran like hell.

One day, surprisingly and unexpectedly, Danka Lipszyc, a friend from the underground school I was attending, came to visit me. She did it against her parents' wishes. It was getting dark outside, and it was dangerous.

We went for a walk. Snow was falling, silently covering the street and the houses with a pure white blanket. This was a new world in disguise. The snowflakes were swirling in the air and resembled little white stars. The houses covered with snow turned into imaginary huts in quiet villages in remote places.

We held hands. We didn't talk. What could we say to each other? I looked at Danka's face: the snow flakes settling on her eyelashes, her nose getting reddish from the cold, her beautiful blue eyes dimmed by sadness.

"I think this is our last meeting." she said, tears in her eyes.

"Why? We live close to each other now. On the contrary, we should meet very often," I said.

She didn't respond, her eyes staring blankly. "My parents won't allow me to leave the house, we have to stay together. I sense that something horrible is in the making. The Germans are feeding us lies, and we are accepting them." Danka concluded, squeezing my hand firmly.

"Danka," I said, trying to console her, "We are young, we

will survive. We will do it together. When the war ends, we will go to school together. What a beautiful thing, sharing life and loving each other."

We stopped walking. She looked into my face and embraced me for the first time. I had never mentioned that word before, "loving." It wasn't in my vocabulary.

"I pray," Danka said, "you're right. You know exactly how I feel about you. I feel so good with you. I am always caught in the web of your dreams. They are very real, giving me hope," she said sadly. "Good-bye," she said, stretching out her hand.

I embraced her, kissing her frozen cheeks. Tears were on her face, mixing with the snow. I was confused, at a loss for words.

"Danka, after this is over I will search for you. I will find you. I will not give up." Suddenly, I felt warm tears on my face. We waved our hands for the last time. I stood watching her close the gate of the house where she lived. The snow kept falling.

5

BREAD

THE SPRING of 1941 came early in Baranowicze. The air was still chilly. The wind brought the smell of wet leaves. The snow was melting rapidly, exposing the blades of the still dormant grass. The branches of the trees were dripping water. Sparrows searched diligently for buried seeds. In this atmosphere of relative peace, even with the hardship caused by the presence of the Russians, dark clouds were gathering on the horizon. There were persistent rumors that the Germans were massing huge forces at the river Bug for a possible attack. Of course the Germans denied it. The deceit was soon exposed by facts.

On June 22, 1941, the German Wermacht, supported by thousands of tanks, artillery and scores of Stukas, smashed through the Russian front, breaking it at many points. The protocol of non-aggression ceased to exist.

Amidst fire and destruction, the war came to Baranowicze. The infamous *Einsatzgruppen*, on the heels of the retreating Russians, swept through adjacent hamlets and villages, killing Jews in cold blood. Jews were then rounded up and pushed into a ghetto. The Germans took a part of the city and strung barbed wire all around it and all the Jews of Baranowizce had to find somewhere within to live.

In the very first month of the German occupation, after the

Russian retreat, Alter Malachowski was taken by the Germans as a hostage and promptly executed. During the blitz roundup, he had hidden himself in a neighbor's orchard. The neighbor was a *Volksdeutcher*, a friend of his and a customer in his grocery store. Sara's father was well liked by their gentile neighbors, some of them even tasting the divine gefilte fish prepared by Zivia, who was known for her excellent cooking. Still, the neighbor zealously pointed him out to the searching Germans: "*Hier Jude!*" This concise vocabulary was enough. The delivered ransom of gold and jewelry couldn't save his life. The Germans took both.

Zivia's family and many others were taken in by a relative with a house at Sadova Street, the main street in the ghetto. Everything except the food and linen was left behind. Kostus was given all the furniture in exchange for helping the family move. Bunks were built and everyone slept two and three to a bunk, nearly forty in one room. Sara found more space in the attic and moved her bed there; other young people in the house joined her, and they built a false wall to conceal it so they might hide in case of an SS round-up. The attic had a window, just enough to get a breeze of fresh air. The window overlooked the street, now swarming with the SS and their auxiliaries, the infamous White Russian police in black uniforms known as Black Crows (*Wrony*) and the Lithuanians in their green uniforms. Through a narrow crack she could watch everything.

By spring the ghetto was in turmoil. Around Purim an announcement was made requiring whoever could work to get an *Arbeit-ausweis* (work certificate). The Jews crowding in the street below were desperately trying to get their certificates. Sara didn't have one. Zivia insisted that Sara should get the coveted document. Zivia couldn't get one because she had to take care of her children. The Jews of ghetto Baranowicze were deceiving themselves, hoping that carrying the papers would protect their lives. Sara was strong for her age, and she believed that she would be able to survive the war. She was going to get the certificate, and if refused, she would come back to her mother's hideout. She slid down like a cat, lifting the secret side panel of the false wall.

"Mama, I am going to get the certificate, I will be back soon."

"Go, go my daughter, God should watch over you."

Sara buttoned up her new blue coat. In her pocket she had a chunk of stale bread, probably two weeks old. During the recurring selections, there was no way to get food and any scrap was valued. Sara left the house. It was night and the street was completely deserted.

Sara already had second thoughts about the *Arbeit-ausweis*. The deserted street was mute testimony that something horrible had happened there. Sara began running, uneasy about the mission she had undertaken. She got closer to the other side of the ghetto. People by the hundreds, confused, disoriented, moving like a leaderless flock, were screaming, crying, pleading. People were being pushed forcefully into waiting lorries.

In a surge of fear, Sara realized that she would have to go through a narrow passage to get to Hovera Street on the other side. This was watched by a White Russian guard. Getting in was possible but getting out was unlikely. But it was too late to change her mind. She accelerated her pace, passing through unnoticed. People around the trucks were waving the work certificates in their hands, which supposedly would grant them the right to life. How mistaken they were. Sara couldn't believe her eyes. These "chosen," with the certificates in their hands, were being herded into the waiting trucks along with children, women, the old and infirm. The furious Black Crows were using the butts of their rifles to force the people into the trucks. Some rifles had fixed bayonets.

Sara was in shock, her childish, innocent naïveté shattered instantly. Somebody was calling her name, "Sara, Sara, where is your mother, what are you doing here?" She recognized her cousin Leah. She was very upset.

"I want to get my work certificate," Sara shouted amidst the screams.

"Sara, go back to the other side of the ghetto, if you can. No certificates anymore, they are taking everyone to be executed, run, run for your life!"

Sara wanted to cry, not knowing what to do. She knew one thing, she had to get away from the roundup. The narrow passage was now surrounded by a phalanx of Black Crows.

Sara began to run back towards the passage. She didn't want to die. The distance was only a few yards. She looked around carefully. The face of the White Russian guard was discernible, blue watery eyes, straight dense dark hair, red fleshy nose with deep pores. Sara was two steps away from the passage but the guard pushed her back forcefully, striking her on her head. She felt dizzy and stumbled, trying desperately to regain her balance.

"You damned little bastard, you can't fool me," the guard screamed. The perimeter around Hovera Street was swarming with people who, probably, like her, were trying to find their way back to the other side of the ghetto. The trucks loaded with people were leaving. Empty trucks were moving in to pick up new loads.

Sara hid herself behind a tall man who was searching in despair for somebody. She took a good look at the White Russian guard. He was in his late twenties, probably a father. There were different rules here. In his eyes not every child was the same. It was now or never. A little light lit up in Sara's head. She felt that she would either die right there or she would have a chance to rejoin her mother. The guard was busy beating someone. Sara darted and began to run as fast as she could. Tears welled in her eyes, tears of helplessness but she ran with a firm determination to get past the narrow passage. The Black Crow's body was blocking it. She pushed him forcefully. The guard lifted his bayonet fixed rifle. He struck her with the bayonet in her right side. She felt a dull pain as the bayonet pierced her coat.

She was free, back on the Sadova Street side of the ghetto. Shots were fired. While running through backyards and alleys she zig-zagged, her strong body light like a feather. Finally, exhausted, breathing heavily, she reached the hideout place. It was almost daybreak. She knocked gently on the boarded entrance to the attic.

"Please open, it's Sara…no certificates, the Germans are killing everybody." There was no answer. She began to pound on the board loudly.

"Who are you?" There was a faint voice from inside.

"It's Sara, open quickly!"

"We cannot because the Germans are after you, they will kill all of us…go away!"

"No one saw me, let me in! If you don't open this damned thing right away, I will call the Germans myself!" Sara said resolutely.

The board opened immediately. She was let in to rejoin her mother. In leaps, she ascended to her attic hideout. Exhausted and drained, she caught her breath. She realized that she hadn't eaten. She reached into her pocket. The stale chunk of bread had been cut in two by the White Russian's bayonet. She kissed the bread before taking a bite, looking with regret at the slashed new coat.

6

MISJUDGMENT

Czestochowa, Yom Kippur, 1942, the day of atonement, a day of fasting. The autumn was bereft of the rustic golden leaves. Nature shied away from this inhospitable habitat. Close to thirty thousand of Czestochowa's Jews were squeezed into a sprawling cluster of dilapidated houses in the maze of narrow streets. The streets even had ghetto names: Nadrzeczna, Mostowa, Targowa, Garncarska. The neglect here was visible, a transient habitat of dehumanization.

The *shul* (synagogue) on Targowa Street was crammed with worshippers. My father, tall, handsome, brown eyes, black hair, in his early forties, prayed along with me and my brother. I was now thirteen, blue eyes, flaxy blond hair with unruly bushy gold curls. I had a small nose, rosy cheeks, not fitting at all into the ghetto surroundings. My brother, Berek, was fifteen, with short, dark blond hair and big brown sensual eyes. He looked much younger than his age. The room was windowless with only a small grated opening close to the peeling yellowish ceiling. Through the opening a shaft of light penetrated the room. The air was stuffy, smelly, causing hardship to the old ones especially. The one day fast had taken a toll on everybody. The ghetto was tense, awash with rumors coming in a tide. Everybody was talking, something ominous and frightful on everyone's lips: *Übersiedlung nach Ost*, forceful ejection from the ghetto to labor camps in the east. What about the old, the sick, the children?

A couple of days before somebody had arrived from the east—he had escaped. His horror stories froze the blood. He vividly described scenes of mass murder, Jews executed by the thousands, thrown dying into an open pit. Nobody believed him, nobody wanted to talk to him, nobody wanted to know the truth. There was no tangible proof to verify his demented stories.

At the door of the *shul*, the blunt sound of a kicking boot. The door burst ajar. Two German *Shuppo* (*Schutzpolitzei*), stood in the doorway, their hands folded behind their backs. They wore bright green uniforms, helmets fitting their heads, black tall boots, black wide belts with a buckle in the center, bearing the inscription *Gott mit uns* (God with us). We stopped praying. Everything came to a standstill. The Germans began to giggle, then burst into hysterical laughter.

"You should pray to your God, but he won't help you anyway," one of the German mumbled, his face getting red. This unexpected visit was a bad omen. Never before had the Germans bothered to walk into a house of worship. Without saying another word they disappeared like phantoms.

We were reaching the final stage of our prayers, the *Neelah* (closing). The weak voices got stronger, like the murmur of a rising sea. Prayers for life, for good health and for survival. At the end, before leaving, we all shook hands, embracing each other, sharing good wishes, perhaps for the last time.

We left the *shul*. The street was deserted. We had a short distance to walk because our apartment was just opposite, at

Targowa 17. After being forced out of Kopernika Street 20, we were living together with my father's brother, Shlomo. He had an apartment for himself: two bedrooms, a kitchen, no bath, the toilet in the backyard. The building was owned by his wife's parents. Shortly before the outbreak of the war, Shlomo's new wife, fearing the Germans, escaped with her brother without any notice, crossing the Bug river to the Russian side. Her whereabouts remained a mystery. Her brother was married too, to a former representative of the Visotzky tea company. She remained in Czestochowa with their two children. One son, Paul Reich, attended Axer's, like me. Paul's sister Ruth had a glass eye. She was about ten, and had blue eyes and long blond hair.

We rushed back home. My father pushed the heavy, reinforced wooden gate. He bolted the gate from inside, a needless precaution. The ghetto had an entrance but no exit. My mother stood in the window, waving her hand. The backyard of Targowa 17 was long and narrow. At the very left was the home of Green, the tailor, who was always arguing with his wife. The window of his shoddy apartment was close to the ground.

"What's going on?" Green asked, lifting the window.

"Who knows?" my father answered, reluctant to get involved in discussions. My mother was waiting at the doorstep.

"Wash your hands," she said, covering the wooden table with a crisp white tablecloth. Her head was covered with a white handkerchief. She was thirty-seven, medium height, with a small straight nose, and the traces of her beauty were still recognizable, blunted now by suffering and worries.

"Any good news?" she asked with consternation.

The Jews in the ghetto were living with expectations of miracles, something which would abruptly change the course of events for the better.

"Nothing really special, rumors and rumors," my father answered sadly, not willing to mention the unexpected visit of the *Schutzpolitzei*. "Do you know, Blima, there is a joke in the ghetto. The Jews have a secret radio station called YWA (*Yiden willen azoy*—Jews want it like this). We are creating good news and we believe in it. I don't know what to say anymore," he added. "Everybody talks about the *Übersiedlung*, but what about our old parents? I cannot imagine them working in forced labor camps. There is something sinister in the whole scheme. It's just sheer deceit."

"I wouldn't go so far, fear always has big eyes, let's hope for the best. I baked a *challah* and there's also a good chicken soup. This time no fish, maybe next year, with God's help. Eat slowly after your fast, don't burn your mouth," my mother concluded.

Surprisingly, the Czestochowa ghetto didn't suffer hunger. There was always a way to purchase food on the Aryan side with valuables. Schlomo entered the room, pale, grim and haggard. He embraced everybody warmly. Schlomo was tall, with dark brown eyes.

"How are the parents?" my father asked.

"They are okay, but they worry," Schlomo answered, taking a seat. The wall clock was ticking monotonously.

"I am tired," my mother said. She kissed Berek and me good night. We went to bed.

"Bolek, are you asleep?" I asked (using our nickname for Berek).

"No."

"What do you think?"

"There is something brewing, I didn't like those two Germans. They knew something, I saw this on their faces."

The wind was howling outside, shaking the roof. Every noise was suspicious, footsteps, the squeaking of the door. We fell asleep.

At one a.m. the lamp post in the ghetto lit up like a Christmas tree. Suddenly the night came alive. Fists knocked on doors. I was the first to jump out of bed, followed by Berek.

"What happened?" my mother asked, still half asleep.

"I am going down to check the situation," my father said calmly. He opened the door, followed by me and Berek. We jumped down the stairs, two at a time. Green was awake too. He stood petrified in a long gown.

"What happened?" he mumbled.

"Don't you see?" my father said, "The night turned to day."

The street was crowded with people, asking questions of each other. The Jewish auxiliary police were everywhere. They went from door to door giving short orders.

"Get ready to leave, every person is allowed to take twenty five kilos, no more. At the final destination you'll get clothing and food. The assembly spot is the old market, at five a.m."

This was it. We got home quickly. My parents and Shlomo packed nervously, at a loss to decide what to take. Not much could be taken in a backpack. The Germans wouldn't allow more than that. When we had left Kopernika Street 20, everything was given to our Polish neighbors with the thinking being that after the war we would be able to recover our belongings. The black mahogany Becker grandfather clock went to Trojanowski. The Persian carpet, china, furniture, paintings to Chmielnik. Piotr, the janitor, who helped us with the moving, got a full cellar with potatoes and coal which were prepared for the winter season.

My mother was sobbing, she just broke down.

"Blima, please stop it, this is not the way to face the situation," my father said angrily.

"I am sorry," she answered wiping off her tears. She was a unique woman, outspoken and usually fearless. "Children, for each of you a backpack, your clothing, shoes, towels, soap. In your handbag you each have a chunk of meat and a can of tomato paste. Put this small can opener in your pocket. Here's some money, not too much, you will need it," she said fighting back her tears. "Keep your certificates in your front pocket." Berek's fictitious trade was metal worker, my trade was gardener, since I had taken courses in farming.

Before five o'clock, still dark outside, we left the apartment, tears in our eyes. We knew that we would never return to that apartment. At the very last moment Berek ran to the attic to hide his valuable stamp album. He was an avid stamp collector. He hid his album between loose wooden boards. He hoped to return home. The war wouldn't last forever. He couldn't envision how wrong he was.

Long columns of people were moving slowly like in a funeral cortege. The columns were growing longer, wider, joined by those coming out from the adjacent streets. People of all ages, adults, young children, babies carried by their mothers. The infirm were helped to walk. The Germans were spreading rumors about labor camps in the east. Masses of people, unaware of their final fate, were being driven like a flock of lambs.

The Germans arranged the departure and selection by street blocks to avoid congestion. Everything was planned to lead us to believe that the orderly departure meant labor camp. The marchers reached the old market. It was deserted. Around the market, scores of Germans with dogs, Ukrainians, Polish police, Jewish police—a despicable bunch of collaborators. At the corners of the market were scout cars with German officers. This wasn't a casual affair but a combat zone, an army phalanx arraying for a battle against unarmed people. The long procession came to a sudden halt. All at once the rear of the marching columns was cut off by a cordon of an SS unit. The Germans standing idle on the side began to move into the center. The whole unfolding scenario was well planned to avoid chaos and turmoil. The SS had specific orders not to frighten the evacuees by excessive use of force. People going to work had to be treated nicely.

The front of the column began to move again, in a rather slow motion. We held our hands together firmly. My father was trying in vain to locate his parents. I lifted my body, walking on my tip toes, trying to get a better view. At close range, for the first time, I saw Captain Degenhardt. On direct orders from Berlin, Captain Degenhardt was in charge of the Jews' deportation to Treblinka. He had even paid a visit to Treblinka to learn for himself about the gas chambers and crematorium. He was surrounded by a group of SS officers.

The pace of the moving columns got quicker and they began to part into two different directions. Women with babies, small children, old, infirm, walked towards Pilsudzki Street, to the waiting trains. The young men and women went straight towards Alley Boulevard, which meant that for the time being they would be left to work in Czestochowa.

Captain Degenhardt carried a swaggerstick, moving it easily to the right or left. Everyone had to approach him for age and body evaluation.

"Now it's my turn," my father said, kissing my mother and us. He embraced his brother Shlomo. He darted nervously, walking straight, his heart pounding. His whole life narrowed down to this moment. He walked towards Degenhardt staring straight into Degenhardt's eyes. A quick swaggerstick motion to the right. He proceeded towards the group waiting at the corner of Alley Boulevard. He looked anxiously towards the old market for the rest of us. Now it was my mother's turn. She was pale, trembling, losing her composure.

"Mother be strong, this is not a time for weakness, be confident so Degenhardt doesn't see fear on your face," Berek said kissing her. I joined him, embracing her strongly. She seemed to regain her composure, she put some rouge on her face to make herself look younger. She embraced Shlomo, who had tears in his eyes. She began to walk towards Degenhardt. Berek and I were trembling with growing emotion.

"Bolek look," I shouted, "It can't be!"

A quick swaggerstick motion. My mother took the left turn, proceeding towards the group destined for the trains. Suddenly there was a commotion in the front column. A little boy, age four or five, had darted forward. He was running after his grandparents. The Germans, confused by this unpredicted event, began to run after the boy. The selection came to a sudden halt.

"Now, now!" I shouted, pinching my flesh, feeling chills like ants crawling on my body. "She should turn straight to Alley Boulevard now," I pleaded with Berek. Berek's face was ash grey.

At that very moment she changed her course, proceeding straight towards the right. The Germans didn't pay any attention to her. Perhaps she came to the realization that the choice was between life and death.

Schlomo began to walk, carrying his small worn little valise. Captain Degenhardt moved his swaggerstick quickly, impatiently because of the unexpected delay. He sent Schlomo to the left. Schlomo turned his head, waved his hand for the last time, and accelerated his walk towards Pilsudzki Street.

Now it was Berek's turn. He looked pale, but confident. He passed Deganhardt without difficulties, holding his metal worker *Ausweis*. Suddenly, for no obvious reason, the selection came to a halt again. Several German officers approached Degenhardt, amusing themselves with casual chat. All the people selected to die disappeared from sight, led out of the market by the guards.

After a fifteen minute break, the selection was reactivated again. Now it was my turn and I began my fateful walk, too young to fear, not mature enough to understand the workings of the German mind. Captain Degenhardt was short, with dark black hair, small foxy eyes, rather Caucasian, a far cry from the praised Aryan type. His face had a deep scar across his left cheek, an alleged code of Prussian bravery, or a mark of a street brawl.

He was wearing a custom made light green uniform, fitted tightly to his petit body. A Mauser revolver was sticking out of his holster. Our eyes met. Degenhardt looked at me at length, somehow amused, a faint grin on his face, visibly surprised to see a Jew with an Aryan appearance. A swaggerstick motion to life.

I passed with relief, joining the group at Alley Boulevard. The assembled group grew to about one hundred people, confused, in a stupor, our eyes searching for our loved ones who had disappeared from sight in a matter of minutes. Some seemed relieved, after passing the test of strength in this dreadful contest of the fittest. I looked around but I didn't see my parents, or my brother, although I knew that they had passed the selection.

A platoon of Ukrainian guards surrounded the waiting group. The guards wore black uniforms and they were carrying old Mauser rifles. These were the nefarious mercenaries of hatred, who volunteered to participate in the extermination of Jews.

"*Schnell laufen,*" the Ukrainian guards shouted.

The lesson of terror began. People were being pushed and trampled by others as they ran. Some lost their luggage, unable to recover it. The whips of the guards snapped into action. The running ordeal for the young wasn't a such a problem, but for the adults this was a super effort, taxing their strength. Some who were asthmatic gasped for air, coughing, their faces purple red, on the brink of collapsing. The ones unable to run were dealt rifle butt blows to make them run. One of the Lithuanian guards was particularly brutal with his whip, as though he was a cowboy prodding a herd of cattle. After every lash he grinned, exposing his bad front teeth. "*Schnell laufen, verfluchte Jude noch einmal.*" He repeated those words like a broken record. These were probably the only words he knew in German.

People were running back and forth like a frightened herd, asking each other for advice. The street was packed with thousands, a stampede. The scene was unreal. The Germans, realizing that there were still too many of us after the initial selection, quickly divided the crowd in two by using the butts of their rifles. I found myself near the center of the crowd, pushed forward violently by the guards. Suddenly, someone forcefully grabbed my hand and pulled me back.

"Stay with me and don't move!" I looked back confused, overcome by fear. It was Heniek Lewkowicz, a distant relative. The hundreds of people cut off by the guards were promptly led to the railway station on their way to Treblinka. Heniek had saved my life.

We ran to Magistracki Place, renamed Pieracki Square shortly before the war. On the Polish Independence Day this was a scene of patriotic outpourings, with music played by military bands accompanied by military parades, called *defilady*. The huge crowds would be the first to disperse; the kids, on the other hand, followed the bands to the barracks. The huge Pieracki Square was paved with uniform cobblestones. To the left side of the plaza was the municipal building. To the right was a small public park with benches and flowers adjacent to Kilinski Street where the Gestapo headquarters was located.

The running ordeal for people who never ran was beyond endurance. Some collapsed, gasping for air, but the repeated lashes brought them back to their feet. The finish line was the uphill ascent to the monastery of Jasna Gora. There a provisional labor camp named Golgotha was established. (The name

Golgotha, not accidentally, was an epithet of the Third Reich fighting the Jews under banners different from the Roman Empire.) Exhausted, we passed the Tomb of the Unknown Soldier, the Polish shrine in remembrance of fallen soldiers. The place was now deserted, no sentry. The eternal flame of the Tomb was extinguished.

Suddenly I realized that my small handbag had gotten light. I looked inside. I saw to my horror that I had lost the precious chunk of meat given to me by my mother. I was left with the tomato paste only. My momentary regret gave way to much more serious matters. We had reached the camp of Golgotha, many on the verge of collapsing. Some stood, bent over, seized by spasms of uncontrollable nausea, their parched throats yearning for water. The Ukrainian guards were still busy lashing the victims. They were joyfully overwhelmed by the free reign of power they acquired from their masters. Some excel in excellence, some excel in cruelty. The youngest among the guards, the champion whipper, approached me, unexpectedly. He stood erect, his hands leaning on his hips.

"Down, *Du verfluchte Jude*," he blurted out.

I looked at him stunned, at a loss to understand the meaning of his order. The Ukrainian guard lifted his whip menacingly, short of hitting me.

"Down idiot, push-ups!"

I didn't hesitate anymore. In one quick movement I thrust my body to the ground. I did it expertly. In school during gym exercises, I didn't have any problem with push-ups. I began my push-ups promptly, counting and coordinating my breathing accordingly. After twenty-five push-ups I was ordered to stop.

"*Gut gemacht, verfluchte Jude.*"

I never learned why the guard picked me. I didn't dwell on it for a moment. The fortress walls of Jasna Gora were quite visible. The monastery, surrounded during the summer by luscious greenery, was now bounded by splendid autumn colors. The bells of Jasna Gora, undisturbed, were calling for the vesper mass.

Each of us received a chunk of bread and a bowl of unsweetened coffee. Many had brought food in anticipation of a long journey. We sat in shock, with bowed heads, after a painful and sudden departure from families. In a matter of minutes families were torn to shreds. The Golgotha group consisted of young men only. The whole group was interned immediately in a former horse stable. Fresh bundles of straw were spread on the cement floor, no blankets were given, the place was only temporary. Surprisingly, I found a friend, a stocky, well built muscular fellow by the name of Joseph Schwimmer. He was a carpenter, confident in himself, not being despondent at all about the awkward situation we found ourselves in.

"If they let us, we will make it," he said confidently,

We found a corner spot in the stable, shielded from the draft. The chill of the evening was penetrating our sweat-drenched clothing. Some were shivering, having lost their belongings during the forced running.

"Joseph, I have some tomato paste. Regrettably, I lost a chunk of meat my mother gave me," I said sadly.

"Don't worry, the tomato paste can be used as a spread, not a bad idea at all, better than dry bread," Joseph answered, resting comfortably in the corner.

"Joseph, what do you think about this whole mess?"

"Jurek," he used my nickname, "I am not trying to think

anymore, it will not help anyway. If they don't kill us, we have a good chance of surviving this damned war."

"Joseph, you're quite right."

"Jurek, by the way, you are in top notch condition. I saw the way you did the push-ups. Everybody was amazed, including that rotten guard. What can I tell you, everyone had respect for you, and so do I. I am sure the guard couldn't do it." Piling up some more straw, Joseph said, "This corner is not bad at all. The horses didn't have problems here, they slept standing," he added, smiling.

"Joseph, we can use our knapsacks as pillows. My father's raincoat will be a good blanket."

Joseph looked at me. "Jurek, you know, you are a good fellow. You are here, but still far away. You are a kind of a dreamer…don't worry, in the end we will make it," he concluded.

The night descended quickly, bringing the chill of autumn. We covered ourselves with the raincoat, not bothering to take our shoes off. The wind was howling, picking up the straw dust, whirling it like a lasso. The straw dust penetrated our noses and ears, irritated our eyes. The straw stalks pricked our flesh, causing discomfort. It was like trying to fall asleep on a teeming ant hill. Joseph was snoring, I couldn't fall asleep. For the first time I was all alone, fighting for my survival, no one to support me, no parental guidance. That day I passed my first test of manhood, twenty-five push-ups. I couldn't fail, otherwise I would have gotten twenty-five lashes. I knew that from then on the Germans would watch me, the way I worked and performed. I would stay alive as long as my muscles didn't fail me.

The long spire of Jasna Gora was looming against the indigo sky. For a moment, I envied the monks their peaceful way
of life, undisturbed by the ravages of hatred against the Jews.
In the wee hours of the morning, the shouting of the guards
woke us up.

"*Los, los, mach schnell!*"

Everything was done quickly. Always in hurry, don't think,
just obey, on your way to work, or on the way to the gas chamber. Before leaving for work, we got the chunk of bread, which
got smaller, and the bowl of unsweetened coffee, which got
colder. In groups of ten, we were led to a construction site a
few kilometers from Golgotha. Huge heaps of sand and stones
had to be moved in wheelbarrows to different building sites.
We got shovels to load the sand in the wheelbarrows.

Joseph and I stuck together. Avoiding the watchful eyes of
the guards, we bought a fresh loaf of bread from a Polish construction worker. Poles supervised the work on the construction site. In 1942, the Germans were intoxicated with their
quick and easy victories. They thought they were winning
the war. New roads were being paved, factories were being
changed to suit the German war machine.

The days of hard work passed uneventfully. A week went by
since the first selection, and there were again persistent rumors
that another selection was in the making. According to the
Germans, too many Jews were left after the first selection, additional screening was needed. The fate of those who left on
the trains was sketchy. Occasionally, a little information would
leak from Polish sources, yet the information was confusing and
contradictory. The Polish train conductors, returning with
empty trains, were mute, afraid to talk.

A young man from Radom in his twenties, wearing expensive high boots, joined the Golgotha group. He claimed that he had escaped from Treblinka. His story was unbelievable, like something out of a horror movie script. These were not labor camps, he told us, but death camps with gas chambers, having the capacity to eliminate thousands of people every day. He unfolded a scenario from Dante's inferno. Unprecedented mass executions under a cloak of secrecy. No one believed his stories: this was merely self glorification; with his bold escape, he tried to make himself important.

The next day the Golgotha group was taken to Krotka Street to face another selection. This time the march was done in an orderly manner, no running or beating. Upon our arrival at Krotka Street, we saw columns forming in a orderly manner. Joseph and I took our places in the fifth row. In the fourth row, a short boy, age ten, stood petrified on a valise to make himself taller.

"You are making me short," I said jokingly, trying to quell his fears.

"I am afraid the Germans will find me too short, this means I am kaput," he remarked indifferently, fixing the little trunk on which he was standing.

"Where are your parents?" I asked, assuming that his parents were young.

"I don't know, they went to the train with my grandparents. In the last moment they pushed me back...I escaped."

A tall man, over six feet, was standing on my left side. He was in his thirties, wide shouldered, with a dark complexion, muscular, an epitome of physical strength. He was the tallest one in the row.

"Attention, Degenhardt is coming."

We all stretched, lifting our heads up. A short distance, away, Captain Degenhardt, the butcher of Czestochowa, was pacing slowly, like reviewing a military parade, accompanied by his body guard, Willie Onkelbach. Occasionally Degenhard's swaggerstick would jerk forwards. A person stepped out.

A human fate was sealed. Degenhardt took his time, pausing sometimes to ask a question, his foxy eyes piercing. Willi Onkelbach was a sharpshooter, trigger happy, a quick draw. He shot with precision with his left hand, aiming at the left eye of the victim. Nobody ever found out why the left eye. Sometimes he killed in rage, sometimes he was very composed. He killed for no obvious reason, just guided by the sport of it. He was of medium height, stocky, red face, with yellowish hair. None of the Jews dared to look into his eyes. His left hand, ominously, rested on his holster.

Captain Degenhardt stopped before the six footer, who was visibly exposed because of his height. While evaluating him, Degenhardt had to lift his eyes up to the Jew. This was too much for Degenhardt, his eyes narrowed instantly in a vicious gleam.

"*Was is dein Beruf?*" Degenhardt asked angrily.

"I am a carpenter and a metal worker," the man answered confidently. Degenhardt looked at him with disdain.

"You are overqualified, too many trades," he uttered angrily. A swaggerstick motion. "Out!"

The man, trembling, his hopes crushed, left the row and walked towards the group destined for Treblinka. Captain Degenhardt was pacing slowly, scrutinizing everyone. Suddenly in one swift motion he stopped. He took one step backwards and pointed his swaggerstick in my direction. I froze, my heart pounding. I wasn't sure if it was me, or the young boy standing on the shaky valise.

"*Was macht die Frau zwischen die Manner, austreten sofort?* (What's this woman doing between the men? Step out immediately!)"

A ray of sun penetrated the clouds. I stepped out, blood surging to my head, my golden, unruly flaxy hair dancing in the autumn wind. I stared straight into Degenhardt's eyes awaiting one single word. Degenhardt burst out laughing, visibly amused by his misjudgment. Willi Onkelback was laughing too.

"Step in," Degenhardt said, still grinning.

I returned to the column deeply shaken by this unexpected encounter with death. At a whim, a human destiny halted at the crossroads. The sun's rays disappeared again behind the leaden sky.

7

A BRUSH WITH DEATH

BY LATE September, 1942, the days of the Baranowicze ghetto were numbered. The recurrent slaughter in the ghetto by the German *Einsatzgruppen* devastated the remaining Jewish population. With the reverberating cry, "*Shma Israel!*," Jews in Poland went to their ultimate fates. The Jews lived by a code of ethics. Their bible was their sword. The handful still left in the ghetto clung desperately to life, waiting for miracles. The young and the brave escaped to the forests to become partisans. Entire families were destroyed.

The day before Yom Kippur the ghetto was closed off after everyone had gone to work. That night, with no explanation, instead of returning to the ghetto, the Germans took the workers to a synagogue on the same street as the ghetto entrance, but a block away. The whole night Sara listened to trucks drive by with the sounds of people crying and yelling. The next day, and for a whole week, they continued to work during the day but return to the synagogue to sleep.

On the very first day the Germans had brought piles of clothing into the synagogue: coats, dresses, shoes, everything. They ordered the women to sort the items. With some of the others Sara started sorting without too much thought, and suddenly she caught her breath. A chill spread through her like nausea as she looked down at the pile. One of her sisters' dresses, a little dress with tiny red and white checks was there, just another rag to the Germans. What did it mean? She didn't mention a thing to her mother; she didn't know if the clothing had been collected from the ghetto or if her sister had been wearing the dress. She held her silence in pain, alone in her fears.

After a week, again without explanation, they didn't go to the synagogue, but were returned to the ghetto after work. Sara, her mother and her aunt rushed home. They found the house completely empty. Nobody there, no sign of her sisters, her grandmothers, her cousins, nothing. They desperately checked everywhere, asking people if they knew anything, heard anything.

The ghetto had been organized, with bunkers and tunnels under the floors of the houses, and many Jews had slipped out of the ghetto to join the partisans, especially the young activists with the Zionist and progressive organizations. Sara's cousin Rochelle, who had been ill, had gone into hiding in the bunkers, and perhaps the others were there too.

Zivia and Chanka contacted the *Judenrat* and after a week and paying some bribes, at last found Rochelle, but she was in jail. She couldn't stand being under the floor and had emerged after six days only to be immediately arrested. She had been crying a lot and her face was red from the constant tears. She was eighteen and was very pretty with thick braided black hair. They tried to get her out, offering more bribes, but nothing could be done. As it happened, a group of partisans had just been caught trying to escape the ghetto, and the Germans were furious. They took everyone out, including Rochelle, and executed them on the spot.

There was no hope for Sara's sisters and grandmothers either. They had been on the trucks. Everyone on the trucks, they learned from a few who had escaped, had been taken out of town to open pit execution grounds and shot. Over five thousand died in an eight day nightmare, a *schita* (Hebrew for slaughter). White Russians from nearby villages were brought in to cover the pits and they described the scene as moving ground—wounded victims struggled among the bodies and the earth above them. Zivia was in a daze, holding a portrait of Rachel, Sara's younger sister, walking around the house crying. There was no time or opportunity to mourn. Sara was alone with her mother.

———

SARA WAS now fourteen years old, grown for her age. Her hair was straight black, which gave her a boyish appearance. She was fearless but her mother was always afraid, complaining, bemoaning her fate. Every day, in the early morning, they joined columns of Jewish men and women, including children ages ten to twelve, led by guards of various nationalities—volunteers, White Russians, Ukrainians, Lithuanians, Estonians, Latvians, all bound by an oath of hatred for the Jews and blind obedience to the German Reich. These outcasts were anxious to serve their masters to the best of their abilities. They were more cruel than the Germans.

Food in the ghetto was rationed. The enslaved Jews couldn't rely on the meager portions given by the Germans. Those working outside the ghetto were able to get extra food from the Poles by paying a very high price. Anyone caught smuggling food was summarily executed. No distinction was made, young or old. The swift death penalty didn't require any approval from higher ups. A guard could do it on the spur of the moment.

Sara, her mother, and her aunt Chanka worked at the office of Otto Werner, the *Gebietscommissar*, (lands commissar). Zivia was in charge of the kitchen, cooking soup for the workers. On one occasion when she fell on a slippery floor badly hurting her eye, Otto Werner's wife treated her, trying to stop the profuse bleeding, a very unusual deed for a *Gebietscommissar* wife.

The group of men and women working for the *Gebietscommissar* would leave the ghetto at dawn. The chilly wind blew mercilessly. Dark clouds covered the sky, sailing from darkness to darkness. A guard, Jan Grabowski, a *Volksdeutscher*, escorted the group. He had round eyeglasses and was short and stocky, bow-legged, with a long curling mustache. He wore a long winter coat. A Mauser rifle hung over his right shoulder. The rifle belt was too long and he pushed the belt forward like the string of a bow. His auxiliary equipment consisted of a leather whip to spur the walkers. Occasionally the whip was a capricious outlet for his moody spells.

The wind got stronger, forcefully sweeping the dust and leaves. The landscape remained unchanged, dilapidated houses, barbed wire, eerie stillness and vast emptiness stretching to nowhere. From Sadowa Street and Szepticki, the column proceeded towards Mickiewicza, where the *Gebietscommissar* building was located. Before the war the building was owned by the Bank Polski. On their way out of the ghetto the group passed the guard post, manned by an old Wehrmacht soldier. The Germans in their widespread conquests were short of manpower. Men at the age of fifty-five or sixty were serving in the rear in a variety of low ranking duties. While passing the guard post, Sara observed a placard glued to the billboard, written in German.

"Mama? Do you know what's written on the billboard?"

"Yes, I know," Zivia replied. "This is a warning to the Jews in the ghetto. 'Those who try to smuggle food into the ghetto will be executed promptly.' This is probably directed to the adults," she added hastily. They had been able to bring food back on several occasions in the previous weeks. Germans were known to adhere strictly and obediently to their orders.

"Do you know of any cases where someone was shot?" Sara asked curiously.

"No, I am not aware of any case," Zivia answered hesitantly.

The group approached the *Gebietscommissar* building. Zivia and several other workers departed from the group, proceeding towards the kitchen. The rest of the group including Sara turned towards the construction site. The Germans were diligently adding to the existing facilities—to them the final victory was at hand. Sara picked up a wheelbarrow and a spade. She transported sand and gravel to the construction site. The job wasn't bad at all. It was much harder to carry a full load of bricks, climbing to the top floor, the legs shaky, bowing to the pressure of the excruciating weight. The German supervisors (*Meisters*), treated the adults and children in the same manner. The job had to be done, no mercy when it came to a physical effort. Hard labor is man's redemption. *Arbeit macht frei*. Sara moved the sand from a huge heap towards the newly erected wing adjacent to the *Gebietscommissar* building. Her job was easy, she didn't have to listen to the barking of the German *Meisters* all the time, "*Los, los.*"

The adult workers mixed the cement. The fresh mixed cement was transferred in the buckets to the building site. Sara was responsible for a steady flow of sand. Others prepared pure white lime from a huge square pool. Since childhood, Sara had been fascinated watching masons cutting out the soft lime like jelly from a mold. She was mechanically oriented, liking manual work, marveling at the workers on the construction site laying bricks one by one on a wet cement layer and then smoothing and scooping the surplus cement with a trowel. The walls were growing amazingly quickly. They did it swiftly and dexterously.

She wheeled the wheelbarrow, pushing it hard to the construction site, still immersed in her thoughts. Sara was from a well-to-do family where manual work wasn't held in high esteem. A businessman was envied and revered. "You will marry a businessman." To many aspiring Jewish families, a doctor or lawyer was beyond their reach. The lunch hour was getting closer, another day of wretched life, but still a life, with glimmering hope of survival.

Sara's grandfather was a *Zaddik*, devoted for life to the Torah and worship. He was a *Talmid Chacham* (student of wisdom). Since the beginning of time the Jews had searched for the font of wisdom. During wintery snowy days he would tell her stories imbued with miracles. The Jews survived the pogroms of Bogdan Chmielintzky and Petlura. She recalled the big samovar humming monotonously, bringing images back to life from the past. God was harsh to Jews, but He brought them salvation and deliverance at the very threshold of their doom. Often an invisible hand pushed them back to life from the brink of death. For the first time she prayed for a miracle. Her childhood was passing before her very eyes. She felt deprived, violated. Why did the Germans kill her father? Why did they have to do it? Why the killing of innocent people? Does it bring happiness to the killers? What was wrong with them? Why did the Germans hate so much?

A shrieking whistle announced a thirty minute break. Sara ran towards the kitchen. The kitchen was bustling, workers forming a line to get their soup. The place was warm, resounding with questions, good news, bad news, igniting hopes and fears. The shattered Russian front was stabilizing. Marshal Vorosilov was counterattacking with the looming approach of "General Winter." Names of big tank battles flew in the air: Kursk, Smolensk, Stalingrad.

"What's for today?" Sara asked her mother, ready for the soup.

"Potatoes, onions and cabbage," Zivia replied, quite busy, making an effort to reduce the line of hungry people.

Sara wasn't really fond of any kind of soup, but she was hungry. The aversion to soup stemmed from forced feeding when she was a little child; now things were different: a slice of bread and a plate of soup were a survival kit to be cherished. There were no benches in the kitchen so some took their lunch outside, some sat leaning with their backs against the wall, engaged in conversation. Zivia brought Sara a steaming bowl of soup.

"Eat, eat, if you want you can have some more, I am sure you are hungry," Zivia said, consternation in her voice.

"No, I don't need more, you know I am not a big soup

eater," Sara replied firmly. Zivia stood motionless, dejected, looking at every movement of Sara's spoon. She was always like this, watching, her gaze landing on Sara's mouth. "Eat, eat," the same sentence, half demand, half pleading. "I'll give you more."

"Sara, when you finish, you will go back to the ghetto. I bought some food," Zivia, added, handing her a little hand-bag.

"All by myself?" Sara asked, stunned.

"Don't worry, I spoke to Grabowski, he will escort you to the ghetto. I mentioned that you have fever and you need rest."

Zivia left. Sara didn't ask any more questions, for a split second her thoughts went to the huge billboard erected next to the ghetto gate. Somehow she couldn't comprehend the idea of walking alone with a German guard to the ghetto gate, even though he was generally very nice to Zivia because she cooked special things for him. She left the kitchen premises looking for Grabowski. Grabowski was walking slowly towards the kitchen, looking for her. She joined him without saying a word. The Germans didn't communicate with Jews. Grabowski walked on the sidewalk. Sara walked on the road paved with cobblestones. The road was for horsecarts, animals and prisoners of any kind. The handbag was light, she didn't bother to look inside, probably sugar, butter and honey. Those specialties were hardly available unless you had money and the right connections. The distance from the *Gebietscommissar* to the ghetto was quite short. The air was clear and crisp. All around desolation, almost an extinct town, once full of life.

The ghetto gate was getting closer. The guard's silhouette

visible. Sara's heart was pounding from emotion. The huge placard was still there. Grabowski came to a halt about twenty yards before the gate. The ghetto gate was very narrow, just enough for one person. This way the guard could scrutinize every person entering the ghetto. This was the same guard they had seen in the morning. He was in his sixties, medium size, a round face with a dull expression.

"*Was hast Du hier?* (What do you have here?)," the guard said tersely, pointing at her handbag. Sara couldn't find the appropriate wording to answer his question. She didn't think that the guard would stop her.

"*Essen, essen,*" she blurted out.

"Come with me," he ordered. He pointed the barrel of his rifle towards her.

Next to the gate was a little dilapidated wood shack. In the back of it on the ground, several bodies lay, probably executed some hours ago. There was a body of a man, a woman and a boy, no more than ten. The boy was shot through his head. His long blond hair was coagulated with blood and covered his face. Next to him, spilled potatoes and a loaf of bread. This was it. Sara knew she was going to die. She just couldn't believe it, how foolish and unrealistic her mother was in her zeal to get extra food. The whole idea was crazy.

The German guard walked behind Sara's back, poking her with the barrel of his rifle.

"*Stehn bleiben* (halt)."

Sara froze. The German guard grabbed her handbag forcefully and turned it over with a swift movement. The contents of the handbag spilled on the ground. She was right, nothing more than a small package of sugar, a jar of honey, and butter.

The guard was mad, his face pale. He pointed the barrel of his rifle towards her.

"Do you know what's written on the billboard?"

"No, I don't know."

"Do you understand what I am talking to you about?"

"Yes, I understand what you are saying, but I cannot read German."

"Do you have parents?"

She quickly understood the trap. "No, I am all alone, I don't have parents. I got a treat from an elderly Polish woman. I don't know her," Sara lied. "I don't have any money," she pulled out her empty pockets.

"Do you see the dead bodies on the ground?" he said tersely.

"Yes, I see them."

"I killed them just one hour ago, probably a family, I don't care. *Befehl ist ein Befehl* (Order is an order). What shall I do with you?" He looked at her, his anger somehow subsiding. Life came to a standstill. "*Lauf, mach schnell, Du verfluchte Jude.*"

Sara jumped out. She was running like never before, waiting for the forthcoming shot in her back. The German guard wasn't supposed to act differently, an order was an order. He had done it before. She reached her house on Sadowa Street in a matter of minutes. Her hands were shaking, she could hardly open the door. As soon as she entered she slammed the door forcefully behind her, turning the lock twice. She hid under the bed, her body shivering and trembling from fear. This was her closest encounter with death. She decided not to leave until her mother arrived.

Grabowski had seen everything the very moment he left her. He saw her being arrested. The following stage was an execution, but he didn't hear the shot. Even if he had wanted to he couldn't intervene to save a Jew. Grabowski walked into the kitchen. He gave the bad news to Zivia and her sister. Zivia was on the verge of collapsing, crying hysterically "What did I do to my dear daughter, I shouldn't have sent her, I will never forgive myself!" On her way home Zivia was sobbing and whining uncontrollably, supported by her older sister, who had consented to the idea of smuggling food into the ghetto. The moment Zivia unlocked the door, Sara was there waiting, trembling in fear. The horrifying scene of the killings had left an indelible mark on her, especially that of the blond boy, who was her age. When Sara crawled out from under the bed, Zivia fainted from emotion.

8

ESCAPE

BARANOWICZE GHETTO, autumn 1942. Summer had passed quickly and with it the days of unattended school. Jewish children were deprived of school, the *Untermenschen* weren't destined for basic education but for a life of drudgery and degradation. The blowing wind twirled leaves swept from forbidden places beyond the barbed wire. The trees seen from far away seduced the eyes and inflamed the imagination. They bespoke the presence of still existing freedom. Occasionally a leaf got caught on the spike of barbed wire, fluttering helplessly like a butterfly caught in a net.

Chanka was in her forties, a woman of strong character, determined, independent, just the opposite of her sister Zivia. Chanka was attractive, vibrant, romantic. When she married her husband Osher, he was in his late thirties and she was eighteen.

Their son Mordechai, known as Motzik, who was Sara's age, worked at the railroad station under the supervision of the Todt unit (Todt was the Nazi Minister of Labor). Osher had been a prosperous merchant in wholesale grocery and hardware. After the crash of 1928, the year Motzik was born, he lost everything. With the unwavering support of his wife, though, he was able to put all the pieces back together, and more than that, he embarked on bold new ventures. He acquired gas stations located in Reitanov, Kleck and Baranowicze. Osher was a high flyer, constantly exploring new opportunities, new ways to expand his assets. Then, in the final days of Reitanov, before the *Einsatzgruppen* entered it in 1941, Osher was hacked to death by his own workers.

At his father's death Motzik was thirteen. He escaped from his home in Reitanov, chased by dogs and beaten by White Russian peasants, and he arrived at Zivia's house, wounded and exhausted, with open sores on his feet. Reitanov was a small hamlet not far from Baranowicze. Chanka and Rochelle joined him later, after learning of Osher's tragic death.

After the liquidation of the ghetto, Chanka decided to go to the partisans herself and tried to escape with some men. The daring idea ended in fiasco. They lost their way in the dark and were spotted near the aerodrome. Two men in her group were shot during the escape and one was apprehended and executed. Chanka wasn't recognized. She hid and changed the man's clothing she was wearing to a peasant dress, managing to sneak back into the work group. She decided she wouldn't try again without what remained of the family: her son, her sister and her niece.

A group of tired workers had just arrived in the kitchen building. Chanka and Zivia were standing next to the huge steaming cooking kettles, long ladles in their hands.

"Chanka, look who is coming," Zivia said, pointing at the approaching men. The two young men were the Kudevitzki brothers, distant cousins. They looked haggard, despondent, with pallid faces and dimmed eyes. They held in their hands tin soup bowls and handmade wooden spoons. Chanka greeted them warmly.

"You look worried," Chanka said with consternation.

"No, no we are just tired," Schmuel, the oldest one answered.

"But still, something seems to be bothering you," Chanka insisted. There was no answer. "Can I ask you a question?" she asked point blank.

"Yes, go ahead," answered Berl.

"Not here, let's step outside. Zivia, take over, I will be right back." They left the building. The chill of late autumn was in the air. Chanka turned to Schmuel. "Tell me the truth, have you ever considered an escape?" she asked him, looking into his eyes.

"No, no, it never crossed my mind." He began laughing. "Escape?" he repeated, stunned. "Escape to where, escape to whom?" He was visibly angry. "There is no one outside to help, a bunch of informers, murderers, Jew haters, or the forest with sub zero temperatures in winter. Nonsense, I am not ready for that, everything is lost." His words poured out in anger. "What choice do we have?"

"Schmuel," interrupted Chanka, "I agree with you, but there is still a chance, but here, this is the end."

"I am sorry, I see no chance," he answered brusquely. "Our family is gone and now we are next."

"Schmuel, please come to your senses, you are young and strong and so is your brother," Chanka pleaded. "It's not too late, I have some money, we can buy arms, join the partisans and fight the damned Germans, kill them for what they have done to us and our families."

Schmuel was unmoved and he answered sarcastically, "You are a brave woman, but it's too late. We are doomed to die. We know it, the Germans know it."

They left. Chanka stood there in silence. Her eyes wandered to the distant horizon that hid a promise of life. She would escape because there was a chance to save lives. At least to die in dignity, not in an open pit, but fighting back. The Germans are cowards—to kill babies and women is easy. They know it. With the Jews the Germans had a very easy job, no resistance. The Jews were overwhelmed by the fear of death, and had lost their desire for living. The fear took control over weak and passive minds. The fate of the remaining Jews was sealed. Chanka returned to the kitchen.

"I was worried about you," Zivia said nervously.

"Stop it, you always worry, you never stop worrying, you saw me speaking to Schmuel and Berl."

"Lipnik was asking for you," she said, leaving the kitchen.

Lipnik was a ghetto smuggler. For a hefty amount of money, Lipnik supplied guns, ammunition and grenades. He had found a safe and uncommon way to smuggle the arms into the ghetto. Lipnik disposed of human excrement in wooden barrels outside the ghetto. The Germans granted him special permission to do so, together with an appropriate title, *der Scheisse Trager*. His job gave him a kind of immunity for obvious reasons. On his way into the ghetto he wouldn't empty out the barrels completely. The arms purchased outside the ghetto were covered with rags and placed inside the barrels. Nobody asked questions. The horrifying stench kept people at a good distance. When he approached the ghetto gate with the guns in the barrel, the guards would scream, petrified, "*Mach schnell Du verstunckene Jude."* Lipnik would whip his well fed horse to make the passage into the ghetto as quick as possible.

"I bought guns from Lipnik," Chanka said to her sister.

"Chanka, I am scared to death," Zivia said trembling. "You think we will be able to do it?" Zivia asked, her voice quivering.

"We will have to do it," Chanka said firmly. "You know my husband was hacked to death by his employees, your husband was delivered to the Germans by your good neighbors. We are next to die, in a matter of weeks or less. We cannot and will not go like lambs to the slaughter house."

Zivia was silent. She was scared. As a child, during a storm she would always hide in a closet or under the bed. "I still don't understand how," Zivia finally said in desperation. "Lipnik left me instructions on how to get to the cemetery, the meeting point," she added, taking a deep breath. She began coughing nervously.

"I will leave before you, with Motzik," Chanka said, and then added, "You will leave with Sara a half an hour later. There is still a problem," she remarked. "We cannot return to the ghetto. We will have to talk to Grabowski. I only hope he will agree that we can stay here overnight."

Outside the building the workers were forming columns. Grabowski was counting them, whipping and cursing. He stopped counting and began pacing nervously toward the kitchen. "Where the hell are you?" he screamed angrily, looking for the two missing women.

"Mr. Grabowski, we are here," Chanka answered loudly.

"I've been waiting for you, you are late," Grabowski said, annoyed.

"Mr. Grabowski," Zivia said hesitantly, "we would like to ask you for a favor."

"A favor?" repeated Grabowski stunned. "What kind of favor can a Jewish woman ask from a German?" his eyes moved suspiciously.

"We would like to sleep over in the kitchen," Zivia said, her voice trembling. Grabowski looked at her, realizing the hidden idea behind the request.

"I cannot do it, why should I do it, I don't want to lose my head, I am responsible for every person."

"Mr. Grabowski," Zivia insisted, "the counting is done by you, you can do it, please allow us to sleep in the kitchen."

Grabowski didn't say a word. He left, upset. Zivia was pale, realizing that she had gone too far. Her heart was pounding, she was visibly shaken.

"What did he say?" Chanka asked nervously.

"Nothing, nothing at all."

They didn't see Grabowski again. If Grabowski knew of their intention to escape, he gave his mute acceptance to the plan. As a loyal German servant he betrayed the trust of the German Reich. Chanka and Motzik left the kitchen building at dusk. The gate was locked, the place deserted. Chanka climbed over the fence first. It wasn't easy. Finally they did it. They were fighting for their lives.

Zivia and Sara watched them tensely through the window. After half an hour, they did the same. To climb the fence for Zivia wasn't easy either. She stretched her hands, her feet dangling helplessly in the air. Finally she succeeded. Sara did it expertly. She was a fence climber from her tomboy days. Zivia and Sara wore long peasant skirts, their heads covered in thick scarves pulled over their faces.

They walked on the sidewalk, not on the road. The Germans didn't allow Jews to walk on the sidewalks—sidewalks were reserved for humans only. They left Narutowicza Street. After a long and brisk walk, they reached the meeting point, the Jewish cemetery. Lipnik had given them explicit instructions. The night was descending quickly and so was their fear. The tombstones resembled ghosts. Those in the graves were secure. They laid down close to each other and waited.

"Will Lipnik come?"

"Maybe he is a crook?"

Hours passed. It was past midnight. Sara thought about Chanka and Motzik. They should be close, maybe only a few rows away, lying in wait, their hearts turning cold like these tombs. Jews were blessed by prophets; one of them said, "The time will come, when the living will envy the dead." The time was here.

"Hush, hush, listen," said Sara to her mother. "Do you hear?"

Three whistles could be heard. Lipnik appeared in the darkness. He was not alone. He was followed by three men carrying rifles. Lipnik carried a white backpack. Zivia and Sara stood up.

"I couldn't find your sister, let's try again. It's late, and I will be sorry to leave them but I cannot endanger other people," Lipnik said angrily.

"Please try again," Zivia begged, "don't leave them, I know they're here. They left before us…"

They proceeded further to the right side of the cemetery. He kept whistling and nobody answered. The Jewish cemetery was a big place. Finally, they found them. They all quickly began to walk in single file. The sky was black like tar. They were very close to the aerodrome. Flares erupted intermittently, illuminating the darkness. Suddenly they stopped.

"We are too close to the aerodrome," Lipnik whispered.

He had made a mistake, he had taken a wrong turn. He was leading the group, angry because of these unforeseen difficulties. He was running, his white backpack swaying and gliding in the darkness like a sail. He stopped again and wiped off his sweat. On the left side, looming in the darkness, was the Green Bridge. Here in the vicinity of the bridge the *Einsatzgruppen* executed Jews by the thousands. Some escaped, wounded, to tell the horrifying stories. Babies, women, men, young and old, murdered in cold blood. Motzik looked to the right. He was trembling. His shirt was wet. He stumbled unexpectedly. The ground was still soft. Some dead bodies were sticking out of the ground. Motzik took another step forwards. He bent down. A baby's little hand was fully uncovered, a small clenched fist. He felt a lump in his throat. He wanted to say something, but he couldn't.

They began to move again. The railroad track was visible. Dogs were barking. They passed dilapidated huts close to the notorious Polesie swamps. The station before the forest was the log cabin belonging to a man named Hatzia. After another few minutes' walk, the smell of burning wood penetrated their nostrils, the smoke billowing like a giant feather in the darkness of the sky. Hatzia was waiting outside the cabin. He was six feet tall, with large hands dangling like two flails.

"*Szczesc Boze* (God bless)," he greeted them with visible relief.

"We had a little problem finding our way," Lipnik said, sweating profusely. He handed Motzik his white backpack and his rifle. "Inside the backpack are two guns, grenades and ammunition."

Before he left he collected an undisclosed amount of money. The three men who accompanied him left too, uneasy in the presence of two women with their children. Hatzia entered the cabin, followed by Chanka, Zivia, Motzik and Sara. The cabin was spacious, clean. A kerosene lamp on the table. The glass globe, half black, the wick not straight, slanted, smoldering. The room had a table, four chairs, a clay stove with two burners. The room had a quite orderly appearance. Hatzia was a bachelor. Now they could clearly perceive Hatzia's features. He had deep blue eyes, straight dark blond hair, big ears. His face was pleasant, composed, no sign of tension.

"Are you hungry?" he asked. "Here is bread, salt," he pointed at an oversized loaf of bread. "Good fresh bread, baked today," he said warmly.

"No, thank you" Chanka said, "we will just rest for a few minutes, we have to leave soon, before dawn."

"Is somebody waiting for you in the forest?" Hatzia asked, surprised to see two women with two children.

"Nobody is waiting for us. We have guns, which might enable us to join the partisans," Chanka said firmly. Hatzia didn't ask any more questions.

"Hatzia would you mind if I ask you a question?" Chanka asked.

"No, not at all, go ahead."

"Why do you help Jews?"

"I happen to like Jews, I pity them because of their sufferings."

"But you are endangering your life," Chanka said, insisting on a full answer.

"You're right, but so what?" he said firmly. "Our lives are in God's hands, people have to help people."

Chanka knew there was something more to it than a likable attitude. Hatzia sensed her doubts.

He began in a slow voice, "My father, the load of earth should be light on him, had many Jewish friends. Jews had been living in Poland for many generations, they were a part of our lives, a part of our landscape. Jews fought in the Pilsudzki legion. Berek Yoselewitz was a Jew fighting for the independence of Poland. Pilsudzki was saved by a pious Jew by the name of Zackheim in Baranowicze. When the Cossacks were running after Pilsudzki, Zackheim disguised him as a woman. He gave him a stool to milk a cow. After Poland chased out the *Moskale* (Russians), Pilsudzki gave Zackheim a gift, the prestigious building of the state gymnasium at the corner of Wilenska and Szosowa. Not just once was Zackheim invited to Belvedere Palace, as a guest of honor. With Pilsudzki's ascent to power, Zackheim, a poor Jew, acquired a measure of dignity," Hatzia concluded.

"Well, Hatzia, what can I say, I wish your compatriots knew the story you told us now."

"I wish I could help more…two women, two children, too bad," he said sadly.

The flame under the glass globe flickered to the tune of the howling wind. The daring escape from the ghetto was only the beginning. How many more escapes until they would find the elusive freedom?

"There are visible signs of a cold winter. The animals are growing thick fur," Hatzia said yawning.

"Hatzia, how far is the Graiwer hut?" Motzik asked, holding the rifle.

"A good four hour walk," replied Hatzia.

They left the cabin after a short rest. Hatzia stood outside waving his hand. They had to reach the hut before dawn. The narrow, defunct railroad track was their only compass. The track was covered with dry weeds. Sara relieved Motzik of the heavy white backpack. The night was cold, the smell of snow was in the air, maybe just days away. The landscape was changing rapidly to marshes. Just before dawn they reached the hut.

Graiwer had escaped from the ghetto with his family. He was living in a hut, surrounded by deep inaccessible swamps, and high reed-grass. During the summer the soft marshy ground made the place inaccessible and dangerous. Not knowing the ground, an unwanted intruder could pay with his life. During the winter, after the snowfall, Graiwer's huts turned to dome shaped igloos. With the approach of autumn, the air by the swamp was moist and chilly. Vapors were rising from the ground, blurring the vision. Sara knew the Graiwer daughter; they both went to the Tarbut private school. But now there was no time for friendly affection and hospitality. After some explorations, Chanka, Zivia, Sara and Motzik found a hiding place not far from the hut. The swamp vegetation was dense, the reed grass turning yellow with the approach of autumn. There was no way to see a person from even two yards. They decided to stay in the swamps during the day and then to proceed to the forest at dusk. Walking in daylight was dangerous. The Germans kept a constant watch over the marshes in search of the partisans. Their hideout was comfortable, they could sit, or stand up, the tall grass over their heads.

A wind began to blow. The reed grass was bowing and swaying gently and graciously. When night came they began to walk again. Occasionally they would stop to relieve their feet from the burning pain of punctured blisters. After a couple of hours, the walk turned to a quagmire. The tired feet would disobey, hardly moving, sinking in the boggy ground. There was no way to stop. Bodies pushed forward in despair and fear. The ominous shadow of death hovered over their heads. People, left to die, would pray; they prayed, too. On the horizon, dawn was breaking shyly.

The edge of the forest came into view. The coveted forest. They had done it. Nobody could stop them. They ran with their hands outstretched, laughing for the first time in many months. They had succeeded in outsmarting the Germans. They looked at the tall birch trees with awe. Tall trees yearning to reach the sun, the open sky. The place was deserted, nothing except the trees, proud, majestic, like ship masts shooting into the sky.

There was no sign of the partisans though. Zivia began to complain, she was almost hysterical. "Why did you take us out of the ghetto," she turned to her sister weeping.

Chanka didn't react. She was silent, composed, looking anxiously around for a sign of life. In these critical moments she proved herself to be a leader. Leadership requires strong character; she had it.

Sara consoled her mother. "Mama, calm down, you will see, everything will be good. We will survive." No words could console Zivia.

Suddenly, out of the bushes two Jewish partisans appeared. They took Motzik's rifle and the backpack. "Wait here," one of them said, "we will be back soon." They lit a fire before they left.

Motzik and Sara collected dry branches to keep the fire alive. A whole day and night passed and nobody came. Finally, somebody appeared again, carrying a pail of steaming soup. Sara recognized Philip Pinczanski, a friend of her father.

"We haven't reached a decision about you yet," he said, trying to dispel their anxiety. He left without going into further details.

Later they learned that some opposed taking women with children. Obviously the partisans needed good fighters, not two women with children. Many of the partisans who escaped from the ghetto had lost their wives and children.

Chanka looked into the fire, immersed in thoughts. It was pitch black beyond the firelight. Zivia began to complain again, turning to Chanka. "What did you do to us, we will die here. We should have stayed in the ghetto, at least we had food and shelter."

Chanka didn't answer, ignoring her complaints. The flames got bigger. A pack of wolves were not far from the fire. Their eyes glowed red, their silhouettes invisible. The fire was a deterrent. Zivia finally fell asleep. Her head resting on her knees, Chanka fought back drowsiness. Sara and Motzik kept busy filling up the depleting stock of branches. Their lives were again in the balance. Freedom was so close and still far. The right to live, to survive, was in the hands of others. They waited in anxiety. The embers glowed, bursting in a volley of sparks sporadically. The ground was frozen. Their lives had been diluted of substance, no home, no husbands, no fathers.

Pinczanski came again with more soup but no news. After two more days, there was a thundering sound, like an approaching storm. Then explosions and the clatter of machine guns. The Germans, apparently, were attacking the villages in search of the partisans. With the flare-up of fighting, the Germans might take a good look at the swamps. Something was bound to happen. The partisans' command was fully aware that women with children might unwittingly endanger the safety and location of the partisans' positions. Prisoners are inclined to talk.

Pinczanski reappeared.

"Follow me."

They walked silently, with a feeling of immense relief. After a fifteen minute walk, they found themselves in a small armed camp. The partisans were getting ready to move out of their bases. Another escape, but they were alive. The ghetto, the concentration camps, the gas chambers were behind them. In one stroke they acquired the posture of fighters. The sacred mission to fight the Germans was real. They stepped out of a dire present into an unknown future.

9

THE BUNKER

GARIBALDI STREET 18, August 1943. A cluster of sprawling buildings, a square backyard in the center. On the far right a huge concrete disposal bin (*smietnik*). These buildings were the Czestochowa bathhouse. Before the outbreak of war this bathhouse was frequented by townspeople who didn't have facilities in their apartments. The bathhouse was always crowded on Fridays before the advent of the Sabbath. Poland then was still far from the brink of modernization. Most of the apartments didn't have bathtubs, showers or toilets. Wooden latrines were erected in backyards. During the harsh Polish winter the fulfillment of basic biological needs was utterly unpleasant.

With the establishment of the small and last ghetto, the German authorities had transformed the bathhouse into a *Quarrantina*, a delousing center, to prevent an outbreak of contagious diseases which the Germans feared very much. The dreadful word *Seuchenfever*, spotted fever, gave the Germans many sleepless nights. The delousing center had a huge tanker shaped unit powered by coal to generate pressurized steam to annihilate the lice imbedded in the seams of clothes. The blast furnace reminded me of a locomotive. The hearth was constantly fed with coal to keep the steam pressure at the highest point. The level was measured by a pressure gauge. In the adjacent buildings (*pralnia*), Jewish women washed blood stained clothing. Later a hand operated mangle was installed. Beds, pillows, blankets, clothing were disinfected, laundered, ironed and sent to Germany. The recipients were German hospitals, institutions and private homes, to compensate the German public for their property losses during the Allied bombings. In the process of the unfolding final solution, the Jews turned out to be a very lucrative source of income for the German Reich treasury. The Germans' diabolical ingenuity was limitless, creating ever growing resources for the fast expanding war machine. Hair was even being processed and used for mattresses for the convenience of German hospitals and for the crews of the German U-boats prowling the Atlantic.

In charge of the bathhouse was Dr. Henryk Wolberg, a Jew, a former Captain in the Polish army, a known specialist in venereal diseases. Dr. Wolberg had a wife, Vera, and a fifteen year old daughter Krysia. He was heavyset with a thick bushy mustache, authoritarian, used to giving orders and being obeyed.

There were unsubstantiated rumors that Captain Degenhardt was infected by venereal disease. These rumors were never proved or disproved. One thing, though, was well known in the ghetto: Captain Degenhardt had a Jewish lover, an attractive brunette from a well-to-do family. She was executed by Willi Onkelbach when his boss' affair gained unwanted publicity. The Germans, if caught having sexual relationships with Jewish women, could face a firing squad, accused of *Rassenschande* (race shame).

The machine engineer in the bathhouse was David Horowitz, somewhat unfriendly, tall, gaunt, with sunken cheeks.

The janitor of the bathhouse was Marjan Weiner who had an attractive wife named Sonia. Before the war they had owned a perfumerie located on Alley Boulevard, adjacent to the Eden cinema. They had a lovely small store from which the cozy fragrance of exotic perfumes emanated, and there were *Ola gum* ads for condoms.

My parents were in charge of the delousing center itself. My mother was an attendant in the women's facilities. My father, sweating constantly, fed the coal into the open hearth. The heat in the room was intense and unbearable.

The building at Garibaldi 18 was outside the boundaries of the ghetto. The people living on the premises had to have a special permit from the German authorities allowing them to live there. I was still working at the Golgotha camp, near the Jasna Gora monastery, at a construction site. When my group came to the bathhouse for showers and disinfection, I escaped with the help of my parents. The Ukrainian guard searched the premises to no avail. He was afraid to report this unexplainable escape, fearful of severe punishment due to his negligence.

After the Golgotha group left the bathhouse, I reappeared from my hiding place. I ascended the wooden stairs in leaps. I counted twenty stairs before reaching my parents' quarters.

My parents occupied the garret area. The rooms were small, low, with slanted ceilings. A table and two small stools were in the center of the room. At the left side there was a tile stove with two burners. To the right was a huge wicker basket covered with a white linen tablecloth. Next to the skylight window, two beds with blankets.

"Where is the second room?" I asked curiously.

"Guess."

"I have no idea."

"Try again."

"Now I know!" I opened the door of a brown wardrobe closet. "It must be here," I said, still not sure where the entrance was. Bowing his head, my father entered the closet. He pushed the center board to the right. I followed him.

The air in the second room was musty. The floor was littered with books. At once I was mesmerized by the variety of books, all kinds of books: art, literature, science, poetry, medicine, philosophy, Latin and many others. With growing interest I flipped the pages. I felt like an explorer reaching the coveted shores of *terra incognita*. In this inadvertent way I had come across a unique treasure of books, the property of a doctor who had been sent to Treblinka. Thanks to those books I would be able to escape the horrors of reality. For how long? It didn't matter. Every single day of life was a gift from God. The first book was Heinrich Heine's *Lorelei*—Lorelei, the seductive siren, whose sweet songs lured sailors onto the dangerous rocky reefs. I found a book of a Hindu philosopher, poet and thinker, Rabindranath Tagore, *Sadhana*, as well as *das Braune Buch*, the bible of the Nazis. In this musty unventilated room a new cycle of life began. A blessed isolation from the cursed world. I read to redeem myself, to understand the real value of life, unscathed by man's cruelty. The Germans took away from me the beauty of life, turning me into a hunted animal. My escape was an act of rebellion against the might of the Third Reich. I was a little Jew against the laws of the German Reich. I would recapture the lost years of school. I would read and write to test my own sanity, to think and function amidst human insanity.

A large mirror lay on the floor, foggy and dusty. In the absence of a companion I spoke to the mirror, asking questions of myself and answering them; a one man school, I was the teacher and the student. This deluge of hatred would subside, nothing lasts forever. Throughout the ages empires disintegrated. I went to bed relieved.

The days in the attic were filled with joy. The only horrifying thing was the sound of the footsteps of the German guard reverberating in the stillness of the night. One day my father came, excited, a smile on his haggard face.

"Listen," he lowered his voice to a whisper. "We've decided to build a bunker beneath the bathhouse. Dr. Wolberg came up with this idea. An underground concrete wall will be erected adjacent to the disposal bin, which will be linked to the bunker. The access to the bunker will be through the disposal bin."

I was excited, yet stared at my father in disbelief. My mother didn't ask any questions, confident in the feasibility of the idea. The most sophisticated bunker without help from the outside was doomed. The idea was unsound.

At midnight, under the cover of darkness, the bunker work began. Hammers were wrapped in rags to cushion the noise. Dr. Wolberg supervised, nervously curling his bushy mustache. The kerosene lamp illuminating the darkness of the cellar was flickering, gasping for air; the cellar had no ventilation. The dust billowed without an outlet to escape. My father mixed the cement with the sand, adding water cautiously from a metal pail. Horowitz laid the bricks meticulously and professionally.

From the very beginning, Horowitz hadn't liked my presence at the bathhouse. My presence was illegal. Horowitz was afraid, because I had escaped from the Golgotha unit. The Ukrainian guard kept searching for me. Horowitz had a point: one person's safety shouldn't jeopardize the lives of others. But finally Horowitz gave up after many misgivings.

"Jurek, check the street, and while climbing the stairs don't make noise," my father said, wiping sweat from his face.

I reached the top floor and I gazed through the grated window into the darkness of the night. No sound, the street was totally deserted.

"All quiet," I reported, proud of promptly fulfilling my father's orders.

"Good team work," he said, smoothing out the excess cement from the erected wall with a trowel. "Doctor, what do you think?"

"Yes, yes, it looks quite impressive. I only hope we will not use it," he said, immersed in thought. "It will be physically impossible to survive in this place for an extended period of time," he added.

Nobody uttered a word. The flickering hope was suddenly veiled with gloom. For the first time a realistic statement was made about the whole desperate enterprise. The end of the war was still far away.

The tedious work on the bunker took over a month, and finally came to an end. The next day, back in my attic room, I sat on a wicker basket, gazing through the window. The sun was setting in glorious colors. The covered wicker basket was close to the window sill. A fly was jumping around the window frame, fluttering its wings. Her undisturbed freedom was something I envied. At that moment, I would have been happy to turn into a fly. My father entered the room. He was visibly agitated, smoking a cigarette, virtually gulping the smoke.

"Is there something wrong?" I asked in a whisper.

"I just spoke to Dr. Wolberg."

"What did he say?"

"Degenhardt called him urgently."

"Is this uncommon?"

"Yes and no, except that he was told to appear at a late hour."

"Why do you worry?"

"I have some mixed feelings about this unexpected call."

"Do you suppose that something could happen to Dr. Wolberg?"

"Yes, I worry about his safety."

"What can be done?"

"Nothing, but one thing is sure, without Dr. Wolberg the *Quarrantina* will cease to exist," he concluded gloomily.

Suddenly, heavy foot steps sounded in the street. I gazed through the window.

"Father, Dr. Wolberg is leaving the building now, he is headed towards Wilson Street."

On the corner of Wilson Street was Degenhardt's headquarters. Dr. Wolberg was wearing *oficerki*, tall black boots favored before the war by Polish officers. The sound of his footsteps reverberated in the deserted street. The corner of Wilson Street was adjacent to the railroad. On those rails, cattle trains filled with Czestochowa's Jews rolled to Treblinka. Slowly, Dr. Wolberg's silhouette disappeared in the darkness of the night. In a matter of minutes a single shot sounded, reverberating in the street, and then everything went quiet.

My mother came up to the attic, her face pale, her hands trembling.

"Did you hear the shot?" she asked.

"Yes," I answered. "The shot came from nearby."

"It's exactly ten minutes since Dr. Wolberg left," my father said, looking at his wrist watch. "Jurek, go to your hideout," he said nervously. "I am going downstairs to find out what happened."

Vera and her daughter Krysia were already downstairs, dressed up, ready to leave. They were pacing the backyard nervously. My father realized that Dr. Wolberg, before leaving, must have left instructions to his wife in the event something happened to him. Vera's face was stern, reflecting her tormented feelings. The rapid footsteps were getting closer. My father unbolted the gate.

"Vera, Stanislavski is coming," he said.

Stanislavski was a Polish policeman, Wolberg's good friend. Stanislavski was stationed at Degenhardt's headquarters and he probably knew of Wolberg's whereabouts.

"What happened?" Vera asked anxiously.

Stanislawski was pale, breathing heavily. He crossed himself repeatedly. "I saw Dr. Wolberg entering the building," he uttered, trying to catch his breath. "Willi Onkelbach was talking to him, he told him to proceed, then he shot him in the back. I was called to carry the body downstairs, which I did. The whole thing was a trap from the very beginning. Dr. Wolberg never saw Captain Degenhardt, because Degenhardt is in Krakow, he left a couple of days ago, to participate in a meeting of high ranking SS officers. Krysia, are you ready?" Stanislawski asked, trying to regain his composure. "I will try to smuggle you out to the Aryan side, my brother is waiting for you."

They left with an inaudible goodbye. The fate of Garibaldi Street 18 was sealed. The bunker, an effort of many months of work, had turned into a fiasco. After constant selections, the population of the small ghetto was shrinking rapidly. Only one place of paramount importance could save the remnants of Czestochowa's Jews: Hasag (the Hugo Schneider A.G. ammunition factory), known before the war as Gnaszyn, a textile factory. The Germans had transformed the place into an advanced production center, manufacturing rifle bullets as well as ammunition for antiaircraft flak guns. Hasag was also manufacturing the *Panzerfaust*, an armor piercing rocket that played havoc with the Russian tanks. Berek was already working there. Horowitz decided to join the Jews leaving for Hasag. He left with the last group, but there was still another small group set to leave at dawn, consisting mostly of the bathhouse personnel. My father was in daze, unable to offer the kind of leadership required in these critical moments. We retired to the attic. Not a word was spoken. The approaching doom didn't require words. This was the end.

"Jurek, listen," my father said, after an oppressive silence. "You will have to join Bolek at Hasag. I know how you feel, but there is no other choice," he concluded.

My father's words were like lighting from a blue sky. After all these efforts, the imaginary castle collapsed. "What about the bunker?" I asked with growing apprehension. I felt rejected, I wanted to cry, to plead. Why were my parents rejecting me?

"We didn't expect this turn of events," he said in subdued voice.

"But still, you can't chase me out at the very last moment!" I erupted angrily, staring at my mother. My mother was pale, tears in her eyes.

"Do you really believe that we want to chase you out?"

"No, but it seems that way," I answered, deeply hurt.

"Jurek," my mother said, "You must leave this place. We will figure out what to do next, we know that there is not too much time left, but still we will wait a bit more."

I didn't know what to say, I couldn't understand the whole situation. I was fully aware that my parents were hiding something, not willing to tell me the whole truth. My father's face was ash gray. He was smoking nervously, his hands trembling.

"Will you still use the bunker, alone?" I asked after a depressing silence.

"The war is not going to end in months, it might even take years, the bunker is good for a couple of weeks," he said, staring aimlessly.

"Why did we embark on this futile enterprise in the first place?" I insisted on a clear answer.

"I wish I could explain more to you, nobody knew, Wolberg didn't know, now he is dead. There is no more logic to what we do and what we don't. We are all alone, no one is willing to help, it's everyone for himself."

My mother was silent, tears on her face. The tea kettle was whining on the tile stove. Long shadows were playing on the wall. Their hopes were dwindling rapidly. Just weeks ago, they had a goal, a bunker, a promise of hope, an extension of life.

My father lit up another cigarette.

"Jurek go to bed, you will have to get up very early," he said, inhaling deeply.

I looked at his face. He had grown old in the past few days, his black hair had turned silver, his eyes lost their luster. There was so much love and affection between us. He took me on his business trips, always ordering the best delicacies, pastries. He took me to movies. During the long days of summer, we would walk in the forest, collecting mushrooms, enjoying the beauty of nature, both of us marveling at the long shafts of light penetrating through the branches. Everything was so short, almost without a beginning, a beautiful start, lost in a cruel war, a war imposed on us. I looked at my mother, her eyes a deep blue bottle color. The traces of her beauty extinguished. Her love and devotion were limitless. Now she was finished, there was nothing to say anymore, the cruel facts didn't need words of consolation. I dragged myself to bed, devastated.

At dawn I left the bathhouse and the precious attic which had heralded my spiritual awakening. I kissed my parents, crying. I felt that I was embracing them for the last time. My mother left the room sobbing uncontrollably. At the very end she didn't want to bear the pain of the departure. When I left the bathhouse, my father was in the street. He stood immobile, tears on his face. He waved his hand.

I was trailing the group headed to Hasag, walking backwards to catch a glimpse of my father. His silhouette was blurred, diminishing, until it disappeared completely. The bathhouse was deserted.

———

Ajzik and Blima went down to the bunker. They took everything they could, pillows, blankets, kitchen utensils. The food they had was sufficient for six weeks. Down in the bunker the darkness was complete. The air was heavy, musty.

"Ajzik, did we do the right thing?"

"I wish I knew."

"We shouldn't leave our children to their fate, this is an act of pure cowardice."

"Maybe you're right, but this is not our fate anymore."

"Ajzik, you know what I said before, we should try to live together or die together. Ajzik, is our situation hopeless?"

"Yes, I am afraid so."

"Do you think there was another way out?"

"No, if we have to die, I prefer to die in this dungeon than in the furnaces of Treblinka."

"But what about our children?"

"They have a good chance of surviving, the young and strong will survive."

"Do you really mean it?"

"Yes, I am quite sure about this." He embraced her warmly, at a loss to find words of consolation. "Blima, take a rest." He put a pillow under her head, covered her legs with a blanket, then instinctively put his right hand into his pocket. Several days before, Dr. Wolberg had given him a vial of cyanide. He felt a kind of sudden reassurance.

His whole life had come to a sudden halt. Kopernika Street 20, the mahogany desk, the black Becker clock, with the brass pendulum, the wall painting of Napoleon gloomily facing a burning Moscow. Then the war of 1939, mobilization, retreat through Przemysl to Lwow. In Lwow the remnants of the Polish army were disarmed by the Rus-

———

sians. He had almost lost his life, being on a train with Polish officers heading for Katyn, where many Polish officers were executed by the Russians. He could have remained under the Russians but he chose to go back to his family. Here he committed a fatal mistake. He could have brought his family to Polish-Russian territory; if he had, he wouldn't be here right now.

Nothing was real anymore except this very moment. A faint beam of light penetrated through the cracks of the concrete waste bin lid. Blima got up, she was sitting on her bunk. She was shivering. Ajzik covered her with another blanket.

"Blima, are you hungry?"

"No, not at all."

"I could brew some coffee..."

"No, thank you. Ajzik?"

"Yes?"

"I still have doubts about our decision."

"Did we have another choice?"

"Yes."

"I don't understand."

"We should have joined them."

"No, I was afraid of Hasag, to go through selections again and wind up at Treblinka. Our children will survive..."

"Ajzik, hush, I hear footsteps, listen, voices in Polish, maybe we should open the lid?"

"No, I don't think so, let's wait."

After a couple of minutes there was silence again. At night, Ajzik left the bunker to see Dr. Wolberg's room. Everything was intact, his extinguished pipe leaned on the edge of the ash tray.

During the day, they heard voices from the street, in Polish and German. One day they heard a conversation in Yiddish. Ajzik cau-

tiously lifted the lid of the waste bin. There was only one person, pacing the backyard, another one was just leaving. Ajzik couldn't believe his eyes. It was Silberburg, the wheeler-dealer, who knew how to bribe the Germans. His retarded son miraculously passed the selection. On one occasion he unintentionally threw a flower pot from the third floor, almost killing officer Werner. Werner, in shock, screamed like a butchered pig, searching for the would-be assassin. Silberburg was able to hush up the matter.

Ajzik climbed out of the concrete waste bin.

"Silberburg, it's me Ajzik," he uttered in a barely audible voice.

Silberburg turned abruptly in fear. He wiped his glasses nervously, gazing at Ajzik in disbelief. "For God's sake what are you doing here?"

"We are hiding in a bunker."

Silberburg was petrified. He began to walk quickly towards the exit gate. "Ajzik I am sorry, but I have to leave, the Germans might accuse me of collaborating with you. I don't need this. You are crazy. You should be at Hasag, not here."

"Please, wait. I have one question."

"Ask quickly."

"Did you see our children?"

"Yes."

"How are they doing?"

"They are okay Ajzik, I am really sorry that I cannot help you. I left Hasag with ten workers. The Germans took a count, I cannot come back with twelve. My group consists of men only. I cannot include a woman in my group." Silberburg was making a point: the case was lost, no hope left.

"Silberburg, I understand, no hard feelings, I just tried," Ajzik said choking on his words. Silberburg left without saying anything. Ajzik

realized that their fate was sealed, there was no way to escape the closing ring of death. He jumped on the waste bin and slid down through the opening.

"Who was that?" Blima asked anxiously.

"Silberburg...there are some Jews still doing the cleanup job."

"What did he say?"

"Not too much."

"Are there any chances to join him?"

"None."

"Why?"

"He has a group of ten, the Ukrainian guard knows every person in his group. I think Silberburg is right, he cannot jeopardize the whole group because of us."

"Did you ask him about Bolek and Jurek? What about the remaining Jews?"

"The situation is very fluid. The small ghetto was liquidated, only Hasag and the other work camps are left."

They sat on the bunk, their heads bowed in despair, there was nothing more they could say to each other. Blima rested her head on Ajzik's shoulder.

"Ajzik, will we remain always together?"

"Yes."

"Even after death?"

"Yes." Ajzik put his hand into his pocket. He gripped the cyanide vial firmly. He unscrewed the top of the vial. "Blima?"

"Yes"

"Take a capsule." She did. "We will do it at the same time."

"Tell me when."

"Now."

They lay down without saying a word. A thin beam of light was seeping through the crack of the lid, trying in vain to illuminate the bunker. There was an eerie stillness engulfed by the darkness. Outside, a scorching day of August. Garibaldi Street was drenched in the brilliance of a summer day.

10

IN THE FOREST

SARA WOKE up. For a moment she didn't realize where she was. She tried to rub her eyes. Her fingers were numb. Her body ached, her legs were frozen. She had covered herself with her short coat which didn't protect her from the autumn chill. She was shivering and her teeth chattered. During the night she had woken up several times, petrified by the howling of wolves.

Chanka lit a fire. The fire was crackling, sending sheaves of sparks into the air. Sara caught the scent of burning wood and got up from the ground and moved closer to the fire. The flames were licking the charred logs. They brought to her mind painful memories. She loved the forest, but under different circumstances. Her father had been her teacher. He taught her to love nature, the trees, the flowers, the animals. She needed him badly now but he was gone.

Sara's mother got up. She was visibly in shock, almost incoherent. The sudden departure from the ghetto to the forest was traumatic for her. She was thrown into the unknown, without a compass, no direction, still grieving the loss of her husband, her mother, and three daughters.

They were among twenty-five or thirty escapees from the ghetto. Some men had rifles, some had guns. This was a motley crew of desperate men fighting to survive, to stay alive. They were all filthy, covered with lice. The commandant of their group was a young man, Moshe Zalmanowicz. Some of the escapees had been friends of Sara's father. Most of them had come to the forest alone. There was a kind of unconcealed envy when they saw women with children. They were openly opposed to having women and children in their group.

Chanka and Zivia got to work. Chanka put a large metal drum on the fire, filled it with water, and got everyone to strip off their clothes. She threw everything in and boiled away the lice and dirt. Zivia started cooking meals with the little that was available, and Sara and Motzik helped. Soon Zivia earned a good name for her devotion to filling the stomachs of the hungry with the meager supplies at her disposal.

It was just the beginning. Food was a real problem. The nearby villagers were extremely poor. They would slice matches in four to save money. Salt was scarce too, sugar non-existent. The small group of ghetto escapees wouldn't survive for too long without being incorporated into a large partisan group. The danger was twofold: the Germans were keeping an eye on the forest, and bands of White Russians (*Zorkince*) were preying on the Germans and on the Jews.

Once a month or so Sara would go with another girl to a friendly villager to take a bath. Not every villager was friendly. Some were collaborating with the Germans. One time it got dark and they were unable to go back to join the group in the forest. Sara's girlfriend was older than her. That night a band of *Zorkince* entered the villager's hut in search of food. They raped her girlfriend. One of the bandits was trying to deal with Sara. The wife of the villager approached him, blocking Sara.

"Listen, this is a little girl, ten years old," she lied. "She is not a woman, don't do this to a child." The bandit left the hut with a few salty curses. Sara never sought a warm bath in the village again.

The ghetto group soon succeeded in joining the Pugatsov unit which was much bigger and well-organized. The Pugatsov unit was operating in the vicinity of Swiecice-Zaluze, about fifty miles away from Baranowicze. During the winter the partisans dug in. They built elaborate underground bunkers called *Ziemlanki*. There even were separate cabins for couples. Of course these had no doors, just a kind of cave. Heating was done in metal drums stolen from the German army. Wooden logs were burned in these drums. Ferns were abundant in the forest and were used as padding instead of mattresses. Soil and plants were piled on the roofs to make them unrecognizable as shelters.

The partisans' compound was like a military camp. Those in command planned operations every day. Even during the night they would leave on missions, mining rail lines, attacking convoys, cutting off communication lines. On one occasion they killed several high-ranking SS officers by throwing a grenade while the Germans were walking on a village street.

Captured informers or German patrols were executed on the spot without mercy. The Germans did the same to the partisans and their supporters among the villagers. The sense of freedom was overwhelming. The German killers were paying with their lives. Some of the dead Germans carried family pictures. They had done the same to the Jews, killing entire families without any pangs of conscience. The rules of war are brutal and inhumane.

One day, it was already winter, the ground covered with

snow, the Germans mounted a surprise attack. They were on skis, dressed in white uniforms. The marshes were frozen. The German special unit was moving at high speed.

The partisans were lucky to get a warning from friendly villagers. They ran as fast as they could, but there were some unpleasant surprises. A tree lay over the river, covered with ice. As they ran across it like a bridge, Sara slipped and fell in and almost drowned in the river. She was wearing a Russian style hat tied across her neck. One of the partisans pulled her out by gripping her hat. Her clothes were stiff in minutes but they escaped and made camp where she dried off and warmed up by a fire. Chanka was separated from them during the raid and was missing. Motzik was also missing; they had been in the village for a bath and split up during the confusion.

After the surprise attack the Pugatsov unit divided in two. Pugatsov headed east and he took his best men with him. The rest—the women, the old men, and the children were left to their fates under a new commander, Misha.

The Misha group was left with few weapons. They carved rifles from wood and painted them black with coal. These they used to force German collaborators to give them food. The partisans never attacked a friendly village. The discipline and the code of ethics was unambiguous. One of the partisans who had taken a sewing machine from a poor villager was almost executed by the partisans.

On one occasion, after they were left with commandant Misha, a *Zorkince* group penetrated the camp. One of the bandits approached Zivia. She was wearing her husband's boots and the bandit coveted them. He ordered her to take them off. Zivia was petrified, there was no way she could reason with the bandit. He was getting impatient and violent. Sara impulsively stepped between him and her mother. She looked straight into his eyes showing that she wasn't afraid. Her heart was fluttering when she said to him bluntly, "As a fighting man aren't you ashamed to demand a woman's boots? Shame on you!"

He looked at Sara stunned. His wild look suddenly disappeared. He mumbled a few words in Ukrainian, something which sounded like "Damned *Zyd*." He left without saying a word.

Zivia was the only one left with her shoes. All the other men and women were left barefooted. Sara didn't have any shoes. Her feet were wrapped with rags. She got two straight wires from the German communication lines the partisans cut. Rubbing stones against the wire, Sara made the points sharp. From a villager she got a ball of wool. She also made a crochet hook from twigs. She made herself a pair of warm slippers.

—

THE SNOW was melting. The branches were dripping water. The shrill sound of impatient birds filled the air. Shafts of light penetrated the dense forest trees creating memorable images. Cranberries abounded in the marshes nearby. Hazelnuts hung from their trees and were eaten green. The forest flowers were sprouting, shyly contesting among themselves in their rainbow of colors. The squirrels got leaner, shedding their bushy fur, busy munching acorns. The forest was like a soothing ointment to Sara. She was in love with nature. Often all alone, she marveled at the forest which gave her shelter, and had a profound appreciation of the beauty she witnessed every day.

During the day she was busy grinding grains to make flour

with a primitive stone mill they made. She helped her mother in the kitchen peeling potatoes. She stood guard with other partisans, on the lookout for any possible German movement. She carried a rifle. She knew how to disassemble and put together a gun with her eyes closed. She was taught how to defend herself. She built a tent made of twigs and branches and covered it with large fern leaves. On the floor were more ferns, and here she and Zivia would sleep. They finally built a bathhouse with a wooden washtub. The men and women bathed on alternate days.

Sara was utterly innocent, however. She didn't know anything about the sexual aspects of love and was completely unaware of how babies were born. But she felt that she was growing. Her body was awakening. She wasn't a girl anymore. She needed someone who could explain to her the secrets of life. She needed someone gentle with understanding. Her mother and aunt were unavailable, old-fashioned in these matters. So she approached a young man among the partisans she felt would be able to illuminate the darkness of her mind. His name was Poniaczek. He was about twenty-seven, friendly, different from the others.

Sara wasn't disappointed with her choice. In the most gentle manner, Poniaczek unfolded the secrecy and mystery of birth for humans, and animals as well. She was proud that she was bold enough to ask such questions. She came to understand the difference between the sexes. She was grateful to Ponianczek for his lecture. They parted and never spoke again about the subject, and she never regretted her decision.

Not too long after, a young woman in the camp gave birth to a child. There were no doctors or anyone trained in medicine. When her labor began no one came to help. Sara went to her and held her hand. When the baby boy came, Sara cut the umbilical cord with her teeth and tied a knot. They wiped him clean with old rags.

In the forest Sara was friendly with everyone. She explored the forest and grew very attached to nature. But with all the beautiful aspects, the forest wasn't a paradise. The life was harsh and brutal. Not so much the danger of the lurking Germans, but the prehistoric living conditions. The good life before the war was gone. Sara didn't have warm clothing. No socks. Homemade shoes. All the small things in life that were taken for granted were a problem. But the feeling of being free was overwhelming. No barbed wire. No SS guards. No mass executions. No selections. Nothing but freedom.

During the night when Sara slept in the *Ziemlanka* she wasn't afraid of Germans. Her new-won freedom against all the odds diverted her mind to life, to hopes, to survival. The battle weary partisans used to say with a kind of sadness, "The time will come when the spring will come to our street." When hope expires, life expires too. The symbiosis between these two is inseparable.

———

SUMMER BROUGHT big relief. As the front moved closer from the east, other groups made contact with them and a Russian partisan leader joined the Misha unit. Contact was established with Russian military authorities and night drops of ammunition, medicine, food and other supplies began. One day, as they encountered more groups, Chanka came out of the woods from one side and Motzik from another and they were all reunited after the long separation and the pain of not knowing if the others had survived.

On warm evenings, the partisans sat around the fire (*koscior*), reminiscing about their homes, their families. Someone would play guitar accompanied by many voices. The songs were nostalgic, the lyrics pinching their hearts. The songs were all about Russian soldiers fighting the Germans. The songs were about love and sacrifice: "You wait for me, I will be back, keep my love as I do." Occasionally men and women would dart from the ground to dance traditional Russian dances. Some were sitting motionless, staring into the flames. Their thoughts were with their lost homes.

The brutal cold was gone, but the marshes came alive with dreadful swarms of mosquitoes. Motzik came down with malaria. To protect themselves from the mosquitoes, they used to apply to their exposed skin a kind of a black tar called *dziegec*. It was an excellent repellent. No one had colds, despite the punishment of nature. Their bodies were strong, although Zivia lost her teeth from scurvy.

In the forest Sara regained her confidence and dignity. Here, surrounded by protective trees, she was a member of the family of mankind, not an *Untermensch*. In the forest Sara was able to think. There was nothing wrong with *her*, there was something wrong with the Germans. Despite all of this she couldn't hate. People are taught to hate, to destroy. Germans were devils, mindless, heartless—inhuman. People with hearts don't kill. But she couldn't be a judge.

By the spring of 1944 the German beast was limping. Artillery was audible from the eastern front. Stalingrad was the beginning of the end of the Third Reich. The beaten German

Sara, on the left, with Chanka, her mother's sister,
in Lodz, Poland, just after the war.

soldiers were in full retreat like the defeated army of Napoleon. In their retreat they were being punished by the partisans. In the forest, Jews were wielding arms, killing Germans in face to face fighting. The *Untermensch*, despised and humiliated, was a soldier.

One night in the summer of 1944 the sky was illuminated with fireworks. Liberation. The partisans joined the Russian army in their drive to take Berlin. In the bloody encounters with the Germans many partisans never returned to their bases. They were buried far away from home in unmarked graves. They died nameless soldiers of freedom. The majestic forest shrouds their remains in sacred silence.

After nearly two years, Sara, her mother, Chanka and Motzik left the forest. Zivia was given a cow as a token of gratitude by the partisan command, a kind of medal for her devotion to the cause. With a wagon and the cow in tow, they made their way on foot back to Baranowicze.

When they arrived they were placed in the former German military compound and weren't allowed to leave because there was still fighting nearby and there were many land mines. Sara couldn't wait and sneaked out to go look for their house. The city was burning everywhere, the artillery shells had done a lot of damage. She found the house smoldering from a direct hit. Nothing was left, only charred logs.

11

VOYAGE TO HELL

HASAG WAS huge, an industrial complex with barracks for the Jewish prisoners and various factory buildings for the work. I was working with my brother in the *Rekaliebrierung* department where used antiaircraft artillery shells were brought in from the eastern front for final cleaning before being rebuilt. Our job was to pick up wooden cases filled with empty shells and bring them to women who calibrated the shells. These had already been cleaned in a big rotating drum filled with acid in the *Wäsherei* (laundry) by workers wearing high rubber boots and rubber aprons and gloves. The smell of the acid was overwhelming. After cleaning and drying, the shells were moved to the *Lackerei* where they were coated with a kind of shellac. The final cleaning of the inside of the shells was performed by women using *Putzmachines* with round brushes that rotated at high speed. Many women lost their hair to these machines.

In charge of the *Rekaliebrierung* department was a German *Meister*, a former Wermacht officer who had been severely wounded on the eastern front. He was paralyzed on one side, with his hand, leg and half his face immobile. He could hardly talk. He never looked straight at you. He liked Berek for some reason, though, and made an effort to speak with him often.

After a while he would leave his breakfast sandwich, thin-sliced bread with ham and butter, in a wooden box under the the shells for my brother to find. Even though he was always hungry, Berek was a pious Jew and never touched non-Kosher food; I enjoyed the delicious sandwiches with some pangs of conscience.

There was a deputy *Meister*, a Pole by the name of Czerny. He was a simpleton with straight blond hair and twinkling blue eyes, and he hated Jews with a passion. He was noticeably annoyed with the *Meister*'s rapport with Berek. One day when the *Meister* was away, Czerny sent Berek to the *Wacha*, the Ukrainian and White Russian guards' barrack, to get twenty-five lashes with a rubber truncheon for no reason. The victim had to lie down on his belly on a narrow bench and count every lash. I offered to go in his place but was refused. After this severe punishment, Berek was carried out. He couldn't walk, the skin on his back had deep splits, and there was a rainbow of colors all over his body. He was frail and thin, all bones to begin with, and for two weeks he couldn't shower, let alone bend to lift a case. He suffered with dignity and never mentioned the incident to the *Meister*, afraid that would attract additional punishment. There were regular selections of undesirable Jews occuring at night followed by prompt executions.

Hasag, like most war industries, was under civilian supervision and there were no SS units in the camps, just the Ukrainian and White Russian guards under German command. There were two directors. Dr. Bretschneider was the technical director, a Prussian officer with a scar on his face from a duel. He was a typical Nazi functionary, in charge of the *In-*

fanterie (foot soldier) department that produced rifle bullets. This department was huge, with hundreds of pieces of machinery running twenty four hours a day.

Dr. Lith was the administration director. He was always immaculate, dressed in custom made suits, with a silky, thick mohair hat like my father used to wear. He was committed to keeping production at the highest level. He was probably a high-ranking SS officer, certainly a member of the Nazi party, but he did a strange thing. After all the selections in Czestochowa, there were still fifty or sixty children aged six to ten at Hasag. When the SS command learned of their continued presence, they demanded their extradiction. Dr. Lith refused, saying he needed them for odd jobs to help the production effort. They remained.

——

JANUARY 15, 1945. Is it a dream or reality? A heavy blanket of snow covered the ground. The snow had been falling intermittently for several days, creating memorable images. Even the barbed wire, covered with fluffy puffs, lost the accent of cruelty.

"Jurek, wake up," Berek shouted. Berek jostled me with his elbow.

"What happened?" I murmured, rubbing my eyes, irritated by the daylight.

"I wish I knew," Berek said, "The Germans are running like crazy, something is wrong."

The barracks were in pandemonium. The Germans and Ukrainians were barking like dogs. In my dream someone had been pleading, vigorously unfurling a white flag stained with blood. The top of the flag was covered with a mourning veil.

Amidst the waves of rushing bodies was the familiar face of Professor Greenberg, my former lecturer in Polish literature, surprisingly because he was long dead. Greenberg staggered, carrying the oversize flag. He was pleading to have the locked gate surrounded by barbed wire opened.

The reality was that the invincible Third Reich was crumbling. The spearhead of the Russian armored division under Marshal Konev was galloping towards Kielce-Czestochowa, catching the Germans by total surprise. Still, nobody could predict the outcome of this struggle. The Russian tanks had reached the outskirts of Czestochowa. The retreating SS units fought desperately, using their *Panzerfaust* to stop the Russian juggernaut.

The remnants of Czestochowa's Jews waiting to be evacuated were concentrated in three war industry centers: Hasag, Warta, and Huta Zelazna (a steel mill). Miraculously, in January 1945, after the massive exterminations which took place in 1942-43, there were still about five thousand Jews left in Czestochowa from a total of thirty thousand before the war. The looming evacuation gave the Germans some logistical headaches, due to the rapid advance of the Russian armor.

The Jews in Hasag were working two shifts—day and night. At the beginning of the evacuation the night shift was in the barracks, after a night's work. The day shift was dispersed in many locations, spread over miles.

Outside the barracks, surrounded by barbed wire, columns of evacuees were forming. Workers of different departments, *Rekaliebrierung, Infanterie, Werkzeugbau, Labor.* Familiar faces: Alek Ufner, Krak, Fabian Gershon, Mietek Kongrecki, Itzhak Rosenblum, Nadzanowski.

Rumors inflated by hopes were spreading like forest fires, news hard to believe, hopes hard to reject. The dawn of the long awaited freedom was at hand.

The Russians were already in town, but the Jews were still on the Germans' mind. The Russians were close to Hasag, but nobody knew how close. Would the golden opportunity be squandered at the threshold of freedom, for which they had been waiting five years?

Dr. Szperling, the Jewish doctor, stood with his attractive wife Gina outside the hospital barracks, soon to be joined by other hospital personnel. Ever since Hasag was established after the final extermination of the small ghetto, the hospital was supposed to serve the Jews of the labor camp. Surprisingly few were sick, because the sick were executed promptly.

Dr. Szperling was a distant relative of our parents. Now Dr. Szperling and his wife Gina hardly looked at us, with our tattered clothes and worn down shoes. Dr. Szperling had clout in Hasag; he was acquainted with the highest echelons of the German administration.

The artillery thuds were getting closer, accompanied by a clatter of machine guns. The Russians were very close, but not close enough to disrupt the evacuation procedure.

On the ramp, the hissing locomotive was ready to pick up the "expensive cargo" on this voyage to hell. For the first time since the German occupation, the remaining Jews of Czestochowa would experience a ride in cattle trains, under severe winter conditions. The snow began to fall again.

"Bolek?"

"Yes?"

"The Szperlings don't know us anymore," I remarked.

"Why should they?"

"Well, I mean distant family ties…"

"Jurek, you are talking like a child, don't you understand, nobody cares, everyone is for himself, no relationships, no feelings," Berek concluded angrily.

Gina Szperling reappeared again, holding in her hand a couple slices of bread. She approached us handing us the bread. "You will need this on the train," she said looking at us. The bread was stale.

"I see Kurt Stieglitz," Berek said.

Kurt Stieglitz was the Commander of the Ukrainian guards. Before the outbreak of World War II, he was a post office clerk in Bremen. He was fifty-two and he had a dark Caucasian complexion and walked with a limp. Now Stieglitz was running, dragged by his unruly German shepherd.

Stieglitz gave quick orders to the assembled Ukrainians, who began to take up positions. The guards carried rifles with fixed bayonets. Most of them were quite old, in their early sixties. Stieglitz was now in the center of the roll call square. He handed the leash to the guard, parting with his barking friend for a while. In his hand he held a swaggerstick with which he shook off the snow sticking to his boots.

"You will leave Hasag on your way to Germany," he began. He didn't mention the destination. "You are going with us. You should be proud that you will be able to continue to work for the German Reich. We are your saviors, the Russians would kill you because you worked for us. Now to the trains—*aber schnell!*" he concluded.

The columns began to move. Outside the gate, the guards began to prod them with their bayonets. No more fancy talking. The Germans were masters of deception.

The marchers, still in top notch physical condition, were escorted by a handful of old guards. We walked through fields covered with snow. The snow was deep, up to our knees. After years of incarceration, I gazed for the first time at the wide open undisturbed view, no barbed wire to cover the eyes. For a split second I was overtaken by a wild idea—to escape, to run for my life, or death. There were only few old guards around. I turned abruptly to my brother who was walking to my right.

"Bolek, this is our last chance to escape." Berek didn't answer. "Bolek, did you hear what I said?"

"Yes, I heard you. I have nothing to say, your idea is insane."

"Why?"

"Look around you, we are the youngest. There are men in their twenties, thirties, in good shape. Believe me, if one of them tries we will follow. There has to be a first one, a leader, and I don't feel like being the first," Berek concluded.

I wanted to cry, sensing that a chance had been squandered. The hissing sound of the locomotive came from a short distance. If only one could take the first step the others would follow. They might kill some but many would escape. This was the last moment, never to be repeated again, to ward off the approaching doom.

Tears were streaming from my eyes, tears of shame, self disgust and humiliation. I knew that the German bastards would kill us one by one. In the very last moment the remnants of the Czestochowa Jews couldn't stand up with pride to fight for our lives. We were walking submissively, like sheep to the abattoir.

"Why are you crying?" Berek asked.

I didn't answer. Words and tears were useless.

The train was now several yards away, surrounded by the SS units, their guns pointed, ready to shoot. The Russians were engaged in the streets, fighting at Pieracki Square.

The guards pushed us forcefully into the waiting cattle trains, prodding us with their bayonets. The whole process of embarkation took just a few minutes. The SS bolted the cars. The train, jarring and hissing, began to move. Those inside were pressed like sardines, gasping for air. Some in despair were using their elbows to stem the tide of surging bodies. The lucky ones who jumped first took the protective corners. Friendship ceased to exist.

The din of the train was rhythmic and monotonous. The clamor of anger abated, some were moaning. The train had no windows, except a small grated opening at the very top. The blow of evacuation was crushing. The shots of liberation were being heard in the streets of Czestochowa, the moment so close and so far away.

The icy wind of January penetrated through the cracks of the car. Nadzanowski was making frantic efforts to hold on to his swaying cardboard box. He had stocked up on bread. The atmosphere in the train was tense, a kind of brewing hostility among people sharing the same fate yet so far apart. The tight closeness made people mad. *Homo homini lupus*. The unexpected departure brought the reality of Treblinka to our minds. Millions of European Jews went in these cattle trains to their deaths.

Stieglitz's deceptive speech didn't augur good, but he knew the psychology of the Jews. For ages, Jews were strong believers in miraculous salvation, God was always watching over their heads.

Jacob Danziger, the oldest from the Hasag group, was unwavering in his belief that the German war machine needed Jews. *Der notwendige Jude* (the useful Jew). Everybody was reluctant to believe that other considerations might exist. Berek fixed his look upon the small grated window high up. Alek Ufner caught his glance. Before his arrival in Czestochowa from Lodz, Alek had dared to escape from a train heading to Treblinka. He had to put up a fight. The people in the train hadn't wanted him to escape. They claimed that every human cargo was counted, registered, and the trains sealed—an escape would cause trouble for the rest.

"Alek, could you check the window, you are the tallest," Berek said.

"Okay, but you have to lift me up."

Berek and I, using our hands as a ladder, lifted Alek up. Alek took a screwdriver out of his pocket and began to chop off the layers of ice formed around the grated window.

"What do you see?" Berek asked impatiently, swaying back and forth under the weight of Alek's body.

"Nothing at all, fields covered with snow, no sign of life."

Suddenly, someone pushed Berek forcefully. Alek lost his balance and went down.

"Nobody leaves the train," someone shouted angrily, joined soon by other angry voices.

"Here we go again," Alek said calmly, putting the screwdriver in his pocket. He didn't say a word. The chance to escape was not wasted here, but in the fields leading to the train. That chance would never be regained.

Alek was a special person. He had style, a hint of elegance even in his work clothes. He wore a heavy duty paper jacket, coarse, which was stiff and abrasive, as well as wooden Dutch sabots. In a pedantic trailing movement he took a homemade comb out of his pocket. Smiling, he combed his thin hair with quick strokes. He had an aristocratic flair.

The stench in the train was unbearable. A round metal pail in the center was overflowing with human excrement. The access to the pail was difficult. The one in need had to secure a balanced position, clasping his knees, so as not to wind up in the pail, or not to defecate on the close bystanders.

There was nothing we could do, time became irrelevant. The worst was the thirst, and some were licking the ice protruding from the edges of the train. Darkness descended. The wind was howling, freezing our bodies. The locomotive was picking up speed, piercing the night.

"We just passed Chemnitz," Alek said, peering out. "It seems that we are heading deep into German territory," he added.

"Alek, why for God's sake didn't anybody make an effort to escape?" Berek said reproachfully.

"I don't know. For a moment I wanted to run, but then I came to a dead end...fear, that's all, nothing else."

"But you tried to escape before, when you knew that the train was heading for Treblinka," Berek asked again. "Is this different now?"

"No, not at all, it doesn't change the situation a bit. It's tragic, but we're all being seduced by a vision of a miracle, even at the brink of our graves."

We fell asleep. I woke when the train was slowing down, approaching a station. The hissing locomotive came to a halt, the wheels still grinding. Loud voices in German were heard outside. Somebody unbolted the car.

"*Raus, aussteigen, aber schnell.*"

We began to jump out, one by one. Several people were lying motionless on the floor of the train; for them the war had come to an end. They had frozen to death.

"Alek, this fellow in a green coat doesn't look like a German, ask him where we are," I said, shivering from the intense cold.

The man was a *Lagerschutz*, a camp guard. He was wearing a black beret, red triangle patch on the left side of his chest. He was in his early forties.

"*Verzeihen Sie Herr* (excuse me, sir)," Alek approached him timidly. "Where are we?"

"This is Buchenwald—concentration camp Buchenwald."

The sound of the name sent shivers through us. I recalled in a sudden flash of memories the case of David Frumer, who had been studying medicine before World War II. At the beginning of 1940 he was sent to Buchenwald. After several months his family received an urn with his ashes.

"Is this an extermination camp?" Alek asked, his face pale.

"Well, close to it, but not exactly," the *Lagerschutz* said. "People are not dying in gas chambers but starving to death. There is no food here, especially in the last weeks. Germany is feeling the brunt of war. The Germans don't care for Buchenwald," he concluded. His terse explanation didn't require further comment. "The dead ones are departing at this point," he added, pointing at the tall chimney, from which a grey smoke was billowing. "This is the crematorium of Buchenwald."

The wind began to blow viciously, lifting the snow from the ground in round swirls. The *Lagerschutz* left. Nearby a group of inmates wore striped outfits. They walked in a stupor, the stigma of death engraved on their faces. The stripes of their clothes were vertical, with a clownish hat to match, no visor. Some of the inmates had wooden sabots, others wore shoes without shoe laces. They shuffled their feet with visible effort. These emaciated inmates were reminiscent of phantoms not from this planet.

The *Lagerschutz's* introduction to Buchenwald wasn't exaggerated. Buchenwald was a death camp, not for all, but for many. The columns of the new arrivals began to move towards a huge barracks, which was supposed to be a bathhouse. It was too late to ponder the authenticity of the place, or whether the *Lagerschutz* was telling the truth. Poland didn't have a monopoly on extermination, Germany could provide the same facilities. On Polish soil the facilities of extermination were the most advanced, because of the large pre-war concentration of Jews and the proximity of the Russian border.

I looked at Berek. We didn't speak, immersed in thoughts. The gravity of our situation was obvious. Millions of Jews perished after entering bathhouses in the belief that they were going to take a shower. The door was ajar, heavy billowing steam in the air. There was a suffocating smell of lysol. The white steam enveloped the glowing bulbs on the high ceiling. At the center of the hall was a large Olympic swimming pool from which the smell emanated. On the left side close to the wall, was a line of standing barbers, fifteen or more, ready to do their job.

A barking order. "Undress, put your clothes and shoes in an orderly manner."

We began to undress. Out of his pocket Berek took out our mother's photo. There was no way he could salvage the last link with the past. No trace would be left after it was consumed by fire. He kissed the faded picture, not daring to throw it on the heap of other photographs. He stared at the buttons of his tattered clothes. Before he had left home our mother had reinforced all his buttons. Soon the shirt would be gone.

Hundreds of people were standing nude, shivering from the cold. The naked looked grotesque, their penises shrunken, resembling tiny thimbles.

The barbers wore rubber aprons. I sat on a stool covering my knees with my hands. My curly blond hair drew the attention of the barber.

"What beautiful hair, a woman could be happy to have such," the barber said jokingly. "The biggest curl I will save for my collection." On his chest he wore a small leather bag, a kind of an amulet. The barber cut off a curl before shaving my head.

"Why do you need my hair?" I asked in astonishment.

"I am a hair collector. I collect unique hair. When you are gone, the hair will remain. I have a good visual memory. I will be able to pinpoint to whom the hair belonged."

I didn't say a word, realizing that my fate was sealed. My hair fell on the floor. I was overcome by a feeling of sadness. This was a final departure. My mother had blond hair, blue eyes. I didn't know too much about her fate, except the fact that she and my father went down to an underground bunker. I sensed that Berek kept a secret. In Hasag, Berek was saying *Kaddish*, the prayer for the dead.

The shaved heads changed us beyond recognition. External human appearance has much to do with hair. After the barber, we were led to the lysol pool at the end of which stood a man of acromegalic features. He looked like a powerful wrestler. He had long, oversized hands that hung at his sides. His head was small, out of proportion to his body.

"*Jeder einer in Basen, sofort,*" he roared. His German was broken, but he was the one with an unrestricted lease on life. "Submerge your heads totally in the water immediately or I will keep you down until you stop breathing," he said.

There was no doubt that he would live up to his promise. His message was clear and unmistakable. We darted one by one, our penises dangling. Those reluctant to obey his orders were caught by his giant hands. He kept his promise. The lazy divers left the pool coughing, purple blue, fighting for breath.

Closing my eyes, I dove into the pool. Before taking the jump I warned Berek not to take any chances. After we left the pool, water dripping from our bodies, the burning sensation of our skin was excruciating. The acid water turned the skin red. Berek was shivering, his teeth chattering.

The group moved quickly into the shower stalls, hoping to wash off the burning lysol penetrating their skin. The shower stalls didn't have faucets, only shower heads, a bad omen unless the flow of water was controlled from outside. A gush of water came suddenly. At the beginning, the water was ice cold, then scalding hot, both unsuitable for a shower. The shower was just another torture, but a big relief as well—we got water instead of gas. The feeling of still being alive was overwhelming. A day alive meant a chance of survival.

From the shower stalls we were herded into the clothing storage room. The air in the storage room was musty. On long counters heaps of clothes were piled up, no size, the same menu with shoes, a kind of a size lottery. Behind these long counters attendants waited impatiently, ready to serve. The clothes and shoes were thrown to us. No socks, some shoes without shoe laces, no underwear, thin striped slacks and summer jackets, and finally a worn out blanket.

Alek Ufner was beaming, he had his wooden sabots, no need for shoe laces. "We are lucky," Alek said "When I saw the missing faucets, I said to myself, this is it. The *Lagerschutz* didn't lie to us."

Alek's slacks were too tight. "Let's trade," Berek said, handing him his long slacks. The exchange solved the problem. Other inmates did the same thing. I got a striped uniform, vertical stripes. I tried to visualize if the inmates in Sing Sing wore horizontal stripes. The Germans got the idea from somewhere. One of my shoes had a missing shoe lace. Calculating the short span of life in Buchenwald, the Germans didn't pay attention to small necessities. The Hasag group resembled a bunch of clowns. We scrutinized ourselves smiling. After the suspicious bath everything was acceptable.

The guards with the red triangle patches escorted us to the barracks. These former communists, now interned in Buchenwald, had acquired a special status accompanied by other privileges, which gave them a good chance of survival. After passing through a maze of doors, we found ourselves in a big hall, reminiscent of a hotel lobby. If Buchenwald was a hell, the entrance, at least, was psychologically attractive.

I stared around curiously and to my surprise I didn't see SS guards, or dogs, but an inconspicuous hotel lobby operated by smiling clerks, a kind of Potemkin village. The whole sight smelled of German deception, but was still a boost for expiring hopes.

The rear part of the huge hall resembled a bank. The tellers sat behind elevated counters. The inmates to be registered formed a line, waiting to be called, not by name, but just *Du* (you). Buchenwald didn't have body tattoos, just a number patch on the outer right knee, and the same number on the left side of the chest.

"*Du*," I was called. I approached the teller window. A woman clerk gave me a smile. She was in her thirties, round face, blond, with blue eyes.

"Your name," she asked in a brusque voice.

"Benjamin Bender."

"Place of birth?"

"Czestochowa, Poland."

"Date of birth?"

"April 5, 1928."

"Trade?"

"*Metalarbeiter* (metal worker)." I had learned in Hasag that this was a priority skill for the Germans, and with all my papers gone, I took the liberty of reinventing my "career."

"Name of your parents?"

"Ajzik and Blima."

"Where are your parents?"

"I don't know."

"How come?"

"We were set apart."

The woman clerk gave me a piercing angry look. "Did you understand my question?" she asked impatiently.

"Yes, my parents were put on a train and taken to an unknown destination." I had to lie, being unable to mention the bunker.

"Okay, and your next of kin?"

"Only my brother, he is with me."

"Do you have relatives abroad?"

"No," I lied, unwilling to mention my uncle living in Palestine.

She sensed that I was hesitating. "The information is required to inform your relatives in case of your death."

I kept silent. In a sudden flash I realized that the detailed records had a purpose. After the war, in case of defeat, the Germans would be able to cover their atrocities, by presenting records showing that the inmates perished of natural causes.

"What language do you speak?"

"Polish and German."

"Where did you learn German?"

"I was taught in school."

The clerk handed me a card. "Sign your name."

I signed the card, trembling, with clumsy, childish letters. The form had bold printed letters on the right top of the form. *Totkarte* (death certificate). The whole thing didn't make any sense. How can a person still alive sign his death certificate? Why these precautionary measures? This only proved that Buchenwald was a place without exit.

The Hasag group was moved to Block 62, with the exception of the very young, ages ten to fourteen. They went to Blocks 55 and 57. The first thing that met our eyes was the pile of emaciated dead bodies of inmates, like logs of wood, outside the barracks. In the archives of Buchenwald their names were recorded. The ravages of hunger had played havoc with their bodies. The dead bodies were reminiscent of rubber dolls, some looked like plucked chickens with sunken bellies. There was no blood or other sign of physical violence. These poor creatures perished of "natural causes," by signing their own death certificates. The diabolical German mind was precise to the very end.

We entered Block 62. The stench was suffocating, the smell of excrement and sweat. The dim light from a single bulb couldn't illuminate the darkness lurking in every corner. Some of the inmates were walking like sleepwalkers, in a daze, phantoms reminiscent of aliens, or those ferried on the river Styx on their way to Hades. Some were mumbling incoherently. There was an eerie stillness around, no sound, an almost audible rustle of dry bones.

Inmates of all ages were shuffling their feet and staring aimlessly with glossy, extinguished eyes. Some tried to hold on to their beltless pants. The pants didn't have pockets. There were no extras in Buchenwald. During the foiled attempt to assassinate Hitler in 1944, the accused ring leaders appeared in court beltless. The idea had a meaning.

My reflections were terminated by the whip lashes of Stanko, the Yugoslavian *Stubendienst*, the barracks guard, or rather a helper to the *Blockenfuhrer* (barracks supervisor). "I am Stanko," he shouted, lashing with his whip. What an introduction.

"Move to the bunks. I don't want you to stroll like a bunch of lunatics!"

The bunks were on both sides of the barracks, a three tiered accommodation. The top floor was the best, but the ascent required special skill and strength. After a couple of days in Buchenwald, the third floor was beyond reach. The ground floor was the worst. The ones descending from the top, like paratroopers, would hit the heads of their ground neighbors, causing animosity and recriminations. The struggle of the fittest began. Berek and I, using our elbows, secured a place for ourselves. The resistance was weak, because most of the inmates on the bunks had arrived weeks before.

The initial encounter with Buchenwald reality was devastating. The ugly face of starvation was painful and horrifying. Hasag had been a paradise in comparison to Buchenwald. There was really no valid purpose to keep the inmates alive in the small camp. These people were useless, not able to work, painfully watching their approaching doom. The German administration of Buchenwald had only one thing in mind, to starve and to dehumanize the inhabitants of the small camp. The process of starvation was overwhleming. The mind ceased to function, there was no way to cope with hunger.

How do you eat a thin slice of bread? Right after consuming the meager portion the hunger still persisted. Do you divide the slice in two, or three, or do you swallow it at once? All this calculated ingenuity proved fruitless. The accounting didn't work. The temptation to devour the slice of bread at once was irresistible. In the waning days of our starvation we made a wish. The very moment after our liberation we would secure a fresh, round, well baked loaf of bread, a loaf for each of us. We would not slice the bread, but tear it piece by piece to the end. For each one a loaf for himself, no sharing.

I was assigned to work in Weimar cleaning the rubble after the Allied bombardments. Crossing the boundary of the small camp on my way to Weimar, I was struck by the difference between the two camps. The big camp was entirely different, inmates were well preserved, retaining their external human appearance. The Russian POW officers were jogging, half naked, not afraid of the harsh January winter. No stigma of starvation, no dead bodies before the entrance of the barracks.

Later, I learned that the big camp was a political camp, consisting of many nationalities; German, French, Italian, Belgian, Spanish, Norwegian, Dutch. These were the elite political prisoners. Even the former prime minister of France, Leon Blum, was in Buchenwald, as well as Ernst Tählemann, the former secretary of the German Communist Party, eventually tortured and hung on a hook, like a piece of meat, in a torture chamber. This gruesome facility was available in Buchenwald too. After the abortive attempt to assassinate Hitler, the condemned German officers were hanged with piano strings around their necks.

Every morning the reveille was quick and harsh. A shrieking whistle, accompanied by whiplashes dealt by Stanko. He wanted to prove his diligence to his German masters. His presence in the small camp proved that he wasn't a political prisoner. If the whip wasn't at hand, Stanko used his belt. His slacks never went down, because his belly was always full. The *Stubendiensts* were in full control of the meager bread provisions. Theft was rampant, and many loaves of bread were unaccounted for due to the accelerated pace of death. Even after the roll call count inmates dropped dead. They never got the bread, Stanko got it.

The first test of human endurance was to come soon. A roll call in Buchenwald was sheer torture. There was no other viable explanation for standing hours and hours to be counted. Such an exercise could be done in a matter of minutes. The Germans were experts in various nuances of human suffering, this was only one of them.

Berek and I left the barracks on our way to the roll call square. We carried our torn blankets, the only shield against the bitter cold.

"Bolek, I feel like I was born here," I said in despair.

"I feel the same way."

"Do you think we will survive?"

"I wish I knew."

"Bolek, do you remember how close we were to freedom? The day shift was liberated by the Russians and we are here."

"It's true, if we had worked the day shift we wouldn't be here," Berek agreed. "Jurek, don't punish yourself, an escape meant sure death," he added.

"Bolek, look around you, this is not a labor camp, but a morgue, a museum of wax figures. Do you think that our parents are still alive?" There was a silence.

"Jurek, how should I know?" Berek knew.

The wind was blowing viciously, lifting snow from the ground. The camp was on a mountain hill, exposed to Arctic winds. Was this place ever visited by spring? Some inhospitable places are blessed by eternal winter.

The lamp hanging on a lamp post was swaying back and forth, illuminating the snowflakes. The air was bluish, brittle.

Columns of people covered with blankets were drumming their feet trying to ward off the freezing numbness.

"Bolek are you cold?"

"Yes."

"Lets turn back to back," I said. In slow motion we began to vigorously rub our frozen backs, trying to ignite a spark of fire in our cold bodies. "How do you feel now?" I asked.

"Much better."

"I have another idea."

"What's that?"

"At this very moment I am thinking about Palestine: blue sky, sun, sandy beaches."

"You are a dreamer, good for you, I cannot stretch my imagination so far."

"Bolek, do we have a choice?"

"No. Do you know what my dream is?"

"No, I don't."

"To be back on our stinking bunk, this is more realistic."

"Bolek, your wish came true. The SS bastard is on his way."

An SS officer crossed the gate dividing the two camps. He walked briskly, wearing a long winter coat, a swagger stick in his right hand.

"*Achtung!* (attention). *Mutze ab* (hats down)."

The hats had to be removed in a quick soldierly manner. The body count went smoothly, no missing or deceased this time. Occasionally some inmates were not accounted for. Searches lasted hours to find the missing bodies, dead or alive. Mostly, the dead were found in the excrement pools, the huge latrines in the small camp.

The wind brought the sound of a military march. The music was played by camp inmates for the inmates, to boost their dying morale. The huge spotlight mounted at the main gate was searching the sky, sending a piercing beam of light into the darkness.

"Dismissed!"

This time Stanko didn't need his whip. We began to run like a herd in a wild gallop. Everybody came alive, jolted by the thought of reaching the bunks as quickly as possible. The wild gallop turned to a stampede. Everyone wanted to be the first in line to get the slice of bread and the bowl of watery soup.

The pressure on the barracks door was mounting rapidly. Some stumbled in their effort to reach the coveted bunk. The hostility among the inmates was detectable. They were cursing, pushing, but to no avail. The door was blocked with human bodies, no way to get in. I lost Berek in the crowd.

In a moment I saw my brother, his head squeezed in a pincer lock between many elbows. His life was in danger. In order to reach him, I kicked inmates on their knuckles. The idea was to take the pressure off Berek. Only a couple of yards divided me and my brother, and a hand tried to fence me off. Being unable to use my hands, I sank my teeth into the obstacle. The hand disappeared quickly with a scream, followed by a curse in Hungarian. I grabbed Berek forcefully, arching my back like a cat, warding off the mounting pressure. Berek was pale, gasping for air, on the brink of passing out.

"You reached me just in time, I thought I was dying. I couldn't do anything."

We were catapulted into the barracks, sweating profusely. The hunger was excruciating. We finished off the slice of bread in seconds. Berek wanted to divide the slice of bread in two, but I was against this idea. Hunger couldn't be divided into small portions. There was no way to calm down the furious stomach. Some inmates in despair tried to build up a small stock. Some time before, a Hungarian inmate died. Four days' supply was found in his pocket.

The *Stubendienst* in charge of hygiene was Vasil. He was Russian, heavyset, over six feet, with long swaying hands. In this giant body was a good heart, a flickering human spark in this abysmal darkness of human despair. The hellish conditions prevailing in Buchenwald changed humans to animals, but Vasil never used physical force to ensure or enforce his orders. His powerful hands could crush an inmate with one blow. Deadly punishment in Buchenwald was common and accepted. A *Blockenfuhrer* or a *Stubendienst* wielded awesome power. A Gypsy inmate who stole a portion of bread was hanged in the barracks by a *Stubendienst*.

Vasil's heart went out to the very young; for them he always had some extra soup. Berek was among those who shared the benefit of Vasil's generosity. Berek was two years older than me, but in the accelerating process of starvation he looked like a twelve year old. In one aspect, though, Vasil was persistent, unmovable, even harsh. He insisted on us washing every morning. The inmates were afflicted by hydrophobia because of the icy water. His every morning battle cry "*Rebyata nada umytsa* (Guys, get washed)" was flagrantly unheeded. The water was freezing, no towels except our sleeves, which froze solid in seconds. We were petrified to touch the icy water. This understandable reluctance caused some pushing and yanking, but nothing serious. Above all Vasil remained a human and he was reluctant to apply physical force. In the course of time Vasil's battle cry turned to a hollow slogan.

Sunday in Buchenwald was a day of rest, a day to reflect, to talk, to hope. Not everyone shared this view. People ceased to reflect when hunger paralyzed their minds. The harsh times at the small camp formed two categories of people: the ones who tried to divert their minds to matters of spirit, and those talking constantly about food. In the debilitating process of starvation, to talk about ancient Greece and Rome was beyond the boundaries of human capacity, but nevertheless it took place during the short spells on Sundays. During these recurring tests in the field of ancient history, the memory was forced to function, dates were remembered, places, names. The oblivious diversion from physical pain to the domain of spirit had a balming effect, even for a fleeting moment.

Our minds departed on the wings of sheer fantasy. This was an act of conspiracy, an open rebellion against the cruelty of the Third Reich, a desperate defiance of the weak against the powerful. This act of conspiracy proved to us that we were still alive, functioning in this bottomless pit of human degradation. This was the only reasonable weapon against the Third Reich. The extinguished embers of human dignity still glowed. The injection of scholastic values was prolonging our lives—*cogito ergo sum.*

Jacob Danziger talked about gefilte fish, roasted ducks, stuffed cabbage. This lecturing was devastating. The listeners to Danziger's talk would reach a point of ecstasy. Their eyes were wide open, saliva dribbling from their mouths. The mind ceased to exist. Alek Ufner, Itzhak Rosenblum, Fabian Gersohn, and I were ascending on the mount of Olympus, Heliopolis, Persopolis and Forum Romanum. Names and dates were swirling in the air: Plato, Demosthenes, Solon, Seneca, Peristocles, Socrates, Zenon, Cicero, Cato, Scypion Africanus dragging the shackled Hannibal to the hill of the Capitol. Hannibal's loyal slave running after the chariot and shouting to Caesar, "*Memento te Hominem esse*" (Remember you are a human being). The Germans were oblivious to this cry.

12

ONIONS AND POTATOES

THE NAME Buchenwald had a meaning. Whoever coined the name took into consideration the surroundings. Buchenwald in German means beech forest, *Buchen Wald*. The camp was on high ground to allow the satanic winds to frolic freely. The topographic location was selected by Nazi experts well versed in the nuances of human suffering.

A ghastly watchtower stood in the darkness of the night illuminating a cluster of sprawling barracks. The ground was covered with a thick blanket of snow. The blinding beams of light would incessantly search to the right and to the left, crisscrossing the lifeless indigo sky. The high voltage barbed wire covered with snow flakes was reminiscent of a spider web, ready to catch a desperate volunteer who decided to die quickly. Once an emaciated inmate threw his body into the wire net. His grotesque body, like a big insect caught in the web, wasn't removed for days, serving as a silent warning to those still alive. The hands of the victim were stretched out like wings of a bird, failing to embrace freedom. Nevertheless the self imposed termination of life was a final exit.

The main gate of Buchenwald was built in the shape of an arch. Every day, back and forth, thousands of inmates passed through this gate. There was an inscription on the gate, *Jedem das Seine*—everyone for himself. There was never a German face visible, only a staccato barking voice coming through the microphone—"*Mutze ab*," the salute of the condemned to the Third Reich.

The air was brittle, crisp, shrouded in the stillness of the night. From nearby, music could be heard, military music. The Germans were ardent music lovers. The sound of music was quite audible, the *Light Cavalry March* by Frantz von Suppee. The musicians were always dressed in the dark blue uniforms of the Hungarian Hussars. Their epaulets glittered, their mouths steaming from the intense cold. The camp band would play to spur the reluctant inmates to march.

I was drumming my feet to ward off the cold, staring at the swinging lamp post. The wind howled viciously. I was thinking about my uncle in Palestine. Some places have an eternal summer. My eyes rested on an electrical pole. The frozen, naked body of a Russian prisoner was still there. He had been caught while trying to escape. His hands were lifted up, tied with a heavy rope. Buchenwald had no escape route—the only exit was through the crematorium chimney.

A short barking order, "*Los, los.*"

We began to march and the music grew stronger as we passed through the gate. Outside was the German SS colony. The Germans lived here with their families away from the harsh realities of the camp. Little picturesque houses, cherry trees covered with glittering icicles. In April these trees would be dressed in blossoms.

"*Mach schnell.*"

We accelerated our walking pace. I was still part of the Weimar group. The group was escorted by an SS guard and a *Kapo*, a common criminal bearing a purple triangle patch on his chest. The *Kapo*'s face was like an expressionless mask. I knew him already. He wouldn't bother anyone provided his orders were obeyed and executed. His nationality was unknown, but he belonged to the privileged.

The hissing train puffed white clouds of smoke. The fifteen minute ride to Weimar wasn't enough to melt our frozen bodies. Pressed tightly together, we swayed back and forth in a balming stupor. Some tried to catch a nap while standing. The train abruptly came to screeching stop, the wheels of the locomotive still jarring.

"*Weimar, aussteigen.*"

Weimar was the birthplace of Wolfgang Goethe. It retained a medieval character with winding streets in the old part of the town. The old Weimar marketplace was surrounded by houses with high pitched gables and roofs, and many Gothic Protestant churches. Weimar had a huge public park and a monument to the memory of Goethe. Outside the park was the "garden house," a plain wooden cottage in which Goethe used to spend his time during the summer. Times have changed. Goethe wrote about the *Weltschmertz*, the pain of humanity. Now his nation was causing so much pain to humanity.

We got off the train. A group of German civilians stood next to the train. They looked like something out of a magazine advertisment, with red round faces and a penchant for beer. Some were smoking pipes. They were dressed in long fur coats, wearing ornate Tyro hats with feathers. The station was the "slave market." The inmates were supplied for free. The first barking call came right away.

"*Zehn fur Beckerei* (ten for the bakery)."

A wave of inmates in a sudden surge darted forwards. The baker was in his fifties with a big overflowing belly, a long cigar in his mouth.

"*Zum Teufel nur zehn, nicht hundret.*"

I didn't move, I didn't push, it was useless. The bread in the bakery wasn't for the inmates, but for the Germans. The smell of the bread wasn't enough to quiet down the hunger. Then came the next call.

"*Zehn fur Reichsbank* (ten to the bank)."

There were no volunteers. The Deutsche Reichsmarken weren't traded in Buchenwald.

Another barking order. "No *Musulmans*, only the strong."

I stepped out, followed by several others.

The streets were deserted in the early morning hours. Some Germans were pushing two-wheeled carts loaded with their belongings. The war had come surprisingly quickly to German cities, shattering the confidence of the population. Weimar, like other German cities, hadn't escaped the scourge of war. The destruction done by the recurrent Allied air attacks was immense. The Germans couldn't understand why Goebbels' proclaimed victory had the ugly face of defeat. The pent-up hatred wasn't against their leaders, however, but towards the barbarous Allies.

The inmates for the Reichsbank crossed the Bahnhoffstrasse, proceeding to the center of the town. The town's park was close enough for us to see the Goethe monument with a marble plaque covered with snow. Suddenly, from a side street a small cart came rolling on the slippery ground, pushed by a short old man in his early seventies. On the top of the cart was a burlap bag filled with golden onions.

The scene was so unreal, the desire for the onions was so strong, that the whole group came to a sudden halt. We stood, our mouths wide open, electrified by this uncommon phenomenon. One of the inmates unexpectedly darted forward and grabbed a handful of onions. The old man cursed, spat and accelerated his walk, looking behind him in fear.

"*Stehn bleiben* (don't move)," ordered the German guard.

Everyone was still. The guard took his rifle off his shoulder. He pointed the barrel towards the onion grabber, flexing his finger on the trigger. "Onion thief, step out immediately," he ordered angrily.

The petrified inmate moved forward hesitantly, but stumbled on the icy ground. He fell, the onions rolling like tennis balls towards Goethe's monument. The German guard began to laugh uncontrollably, his rifle jumping up and down. "Stand up, *Du verfluchte Jude*," he roared. In vain the inmate tried to lift himself up. "Pick up the onions. *Schnell.*"

The inmate, lying on the ground, crawled a bit. He stretched out his right hand, trying to grab the first onion. The moment he grabbed the onion, the guard pressed the inmate's hand with his nailed boot. The screams of the wounded inmate froze the blood. He was trying desperately to remove the pressing boot from his hand. The guard relieved the pressure a little bit, but swiftly, with his left boot, kicked the inmate in the face. The wounded inmate, bleeding profusely, crawled like a dog towards the monument for cover. He again tried to stand up but the blows came from all over. The guard was hitting him with the butt of his rifle.

I turned my head in horror. This act of bestiality was a clear indication that the guard was ready to commit murder. I lifted my head in a silent prayer, tears in my eyes. I was staring at Goethe's marble plaque, whispering the words of Goethe: *Noble is the human, helpful and good, this is what differentiates him from all the mean we know and we imagine.*

The vicious guard was a killer, breathing heavily, sweating in the icy winter air. Besides being pleasurable, beating inmates was a tedious job. He spat repeatedly, uttered a few salty curses, and corrected his disheveled uniform. He left his victim unconscious.

I stepped out, and after me, two more inmates. They handed over the wounded inmate. His face was swollen, a red pulp, unrecognizable. I took a handful of snow and began to gently rub his wounded face, his lips and temple, trying to revive him. Suddenly the lifeless body quivered, a faint groan came out of his mouth. He was alive.

The town hall clock struck six times.

"*Los, los, verfluchte noch einmal* (quickly, quickly, damn you again)," the German guard shouted madly.

With the help of another inmate, I lifted the battered body. The inmate was light. His eye sockets were swollen, blood oozing over his face. The *Kapo*, who was silent and was watching the episode, took out a handkerchief and gave it to the wounded inmate without a word. After a short walk, we reached the half destroyed Reichsbank. I was still in shock, thoughts crowding fiercely in my mind. Would there be any survivors left to tell these horror stories? Where were the biblical angels carrying the scepter of miracles?

The Reichsbank was in ruins. Huge blocks of concrete dangled on long curved iron rods, the charred walls still intact. We entered the destroyed building. The air was sulphurous, suffocating. Half of the roof had collapsed, strangely leaving the center stairs intact. The place was a total mess, broken chairs, strewn papers, smashed tables, counters, long icy stalactites hanging from the roof. The *Kapo* gave short orders. We would have to knock down the concrete blocks dangling on the iron rods.

The steep stairs had no railings, or any kind of support to serve as a standing platform. If an inmate swinging a heavy sledgehammer missed the concrete block, he would wind up falling, which meant death. The *Kapo*'s instructions were explicit; doubtless this was a tricky and dangerous business.

"You sit on the side," the *Kapo* said, turning to the wounded inmate, who was regaining his senses. "You're lucky," he added, "stealing means death. I hope you remember this for the rest of your life."

After losing the wounded inmate, our group consisted of seven. We would do this job one by one. The first of the group was handed a heavy construction sledgehammer. He was a Hungarian inmate, still in the early stages of "survival capacity," in Buchenwald only a week. He trembled, but he gripped the long handle of the sledgehammer firmly. The stairs were slippery too. The bank floor was strewn with metal scrap, not even a narrow path. Climbing cautiously, he reached the top of the stairs. He assumed a straddling position, looking around and scrutinizing the huge concrete block. Standing firmly, he stepped back, taking a wider angle to hit the block with more power. Again he corrected his position, then he swung the sledgehammer. He hit the bottom part of the concrete block, but the hammer glided over the surface. The momentum of the swing swooped him off. He was airborne, his hands still clinging to the hammer. He landed on a pile of metal scrap, and remained on the heap motionless. No sign of life, the hammer lying not far from him, blood gushing profusely from his split head.

"Take the body outside," the *Kapo* shouted, visibly shaken. "Next!"

The next one was a Gypsy inmate, pale and shaken by the unexpected death. He lifted the hammer and began to climb the stairs. The tense inmates followed his every movement, being quite aware that this sledgehammer job was a life-threatening endeavor. He swung the hammer forcefully, but the hammer bounced back rapidly. With the last stroke, the hammer fell from his hands and went down. The scene was grotesque, the inmate standing without the hammer, not knowing what to do.

"Down you imbecile!" the *Kapo* shouted, angry. "I don't intend to be here a whole day playing with these damned concrete blocks. Who is going next?" he said scrutinizing every inmate.

"I am going up," I said, lifting the sledgehammer.

"You?" repeated the *Kapo* in disbelief.

"Yes, I am going up," I said firmly.

"You think you can do it?"

"Yes, I have to do it and I will do it."

"But why do you want to do it?" I didn't say a word, staring silently at the dead body of the inmate. "How old are you?

"I am almost seventeen."

"Okay, go up." Then he added, "You are the youngest, all the idiots around you are much older, I hope you can do it."

"I'll do it," I said, holding myself erect.

"But be careful. I don't want another dead," the *Kapo* uttered with a kind of sympathy.

I ascended the slippery stairs and scrutinized the huge concrete block. One side was smooth, the other side was rugged. There was a thin crack running across the block, along the iron rod. I decided to hit the concrete as close as possible to the rod. I clasped the handle of the hammer firmly. I swung twice, hitting the crack. With the third blow, the huge concrete split in two, falling down. My body was shivering from the effort. I took a deep breath, overcome by a sudden dizziness.

I turned to the other block, looking down smiling. Again I looked for a possible crack, following the previous procedure, so as not to hit blindly. In the process of starvation every minimal effort was beyond the physical capacity to endure. The three weeks in Buchenwald had taken a heavy toll on me. No one was able to withstand the crushing weight of hunger and retain physical fitness.

After two blows, another block went down. I was gasping for air, my legs shaking, giving up. Berek was quite right, the work in the rubble of Weimar would accelerate our doom. I felt dizzy. One of the inmates climbed the stairs to give me a supportive hand. I was helped down, my legs feeble.

"You are really good," said the *Kapo* with respect. "What can I tell you, you know exactly how to hold the sledgehammer, you deserve a prize."

"A prize?" I repeated, unsure if I had heard it right.

"You will get ten potatoes," he said.

"Thank you so much," I answered, overwhelmed with joy. Five potatoes for Berek, five for me. Another lease on life. The other inmates gazed at me with envy. I really didn't care.

Thanks to my strength and determination I won a prize. I was very proud, and Berek would be happy too.

We would have to decide how to handle the potatoes. To keep them, to eat them at once, or eat them in the span of five days, one potato a day. I knew that the temptation would be strong to finish them off at once. In a struggle for survival there was a need for discipline. There was also the possibility that someone would steal the potatoes during the night.

"Half an hour lunch," shouted the *Kapo*. Lunch without a lunch.

The German guard took out a canteen from his knapsack. Outside the bank in the street, an army mobile kitchen arrived. The mobile kitchen served the Buchenwald guards. The German guard left the building holding his canteen. He returned in a while carrying a steaming canteen full of potatoes, carrots, cabbage and meat. We looked at him, salivating. The guard sat down in the corner of the building. He leaned his rifle on the side, next to him. From his knapsack he took out a whole rectangular loaf of bread. Using a small pocket knife he cut small slices, and with every spoon of the thick soup he took a bite of bread.

For us the same loaf of bread was divided in ten slices. On a slice of bread we had to work and stand up three hours in freezing temperatures to be counted. Buchenwald wasn't a labor camp but a torture chamber. Right here before our eyes this damned bastard finished off a whole loaf of bread in a matter of minutes.

The face of the guard was red, his mouth steaming. He opened his winter coat, being warm. We were shivering like aspen leaves. The guard smacked his tongue a couple times, accompanied by sporadic burps. He lit up a cigarette, discarding the empty silver wrapper, Juno brand. A memory of late September of 1939 came to my mind. I remembered a German commercial:"*Warum is Juno rund? Aus gutem Grund is Juno rund* (Why is Juno round? For obvious reasons the Juno is round.)."

"Let's light up a fire," I said to the inmates.We began to collect pieces of wood and discarded newspaper, *Der Volkischer Beobachter*. "I will ask the guard for matches," I said, leaving my stunned companions.

"Maybe you shouldn't do it," remarked one of the inmates, "You never know, this guy is an animal."

"Well, I will try. He can say no, he might holler, but he will not beat me up for asking." I approached the guard confidently. I looked straight into his eyes. "Could you please spare some matches to light a fire?"

The guard didn't say a word. He wasn't in a hurry to accede to this request. Maybe it was beyond his dignity to talk to a Jew. The guard gave me a slanted suspicious look. Obviously he had seen me knocking down the concrete block. He inhaled the smoke of his cigarette deeply, then without a word gave me the matches.

One match did the job, the paper and the red wood caught fire. I went back, handing the guard the matches. "Thank you," I said.

The guard gazed at me with a faint smile. "I saw you knocking down the concrete block, a job well done," he said.

The battered inmate got closer to the fire. He was in a daze. His face was swollen, the eyes hardly visible, lips cracked, two front teeth missing. He was immersed in thoughts, staring into the flames like a caveman in primordial times. I gave him a look, thinking about his background. What was going through his mind now? He was born to loving parents, he was fed, he had shelter, but now he was nothing.

The flames were licking the wood, crackling in a sheaf of sparks, bringing memories of lost youth. Beams of winter light were slipping through the damaged roof. The ten potatoes were ready, charred by the glowing embers. Well earned potatoes, a prize of human goodwill, ignited by a dormant spark of dying humanity. There was still a ray of hope emanating from the abyss of darkness. The human soul wasn't extinct. I wrapped the hot potatoes tightly with newspaper.

We went back to work gathering the huge stones and carrying them outside the building. The freezing air was penetrating my thin clothes. I made an effort to stretch, my back aching. There was no way my body would be able to survive this hellish life.

The town hall clock struck five times. Dusk was descending rapidly. We formed a column outside the bank. There was rubble all over. The Germans who unleashed this war were paying a price for their arrogance and disregard for human life. Dreams of conquest crumbled and turned to ashes. The sky was grey, the snow was hardening. The streets were deserted, only the *Shuppo* paced the street, drumming his feet to ward off the cold. A short shrieking whistle announced the end of work.

On our way to the train, we marched on a side road. We turned sharply to the left, leaving the road route. We passed through a farming area unscathed by the calamities of the war. A German farmer smoking a pipe stood next to the wooden fence of his house. He was holding on a leash a giant German shepherd barking viciously. The German shepherds were far from being good shepherds. They played a dismal role in Buchenwald.

"*Gruss Gott*," said the farmer to the escorting guards, puffing his pipe. "Please step in for hot coffee," the farmer said, turning to the guards. "Don't worry about this trash," he pointed at us, sensing the guards' indecision. "I will lock them up in the cow shed," he said, smiling stupidly.

This wasn't a bad idea at all, to be shielded for a while from the freezing wind. The shed was warm and pleasant, regardless of the manure smell. The place was completely dark, but the dying winter daylight was still penetrating between the boards of the cow shed. As our eyes got used to the darkness, we could distinguish white moving spots. To our surprise we saw snow white rabbits crunching turnips.

This new situation created a host of possibilities, even for a short time, to enjoy rest, and the animal food to share. We didn't waste any time. Every inmate got busy in his own way. The crunching and shredding got louder with the unexpected addition of the new participants. We found ourselves surrounded by benevolent companions, cows and rabbits. I didn't move, warming my hands on a cow's belly. What a noble animal. Time came to a standstill, the hell of Buchenwald ceased to exist.

Next to me one of the inmates tried frantically to milk a cow, lying underneath. The large and pendulous udder was elusive. He was pulling desperately on the teats, trying to direct the flow of the milk into his mouth. His stubborn effort turned into a fiasco. The cow got very impatient with his lack of expertise and whipped her tail nervously. Further in the corner another inmate, oblivious to reality, was taking a nap. His head was resting comfortably on a cow's warm belly. The cow was in process of ruminating her cud. The cow shed door opened.

"*Raus, raus.*"

The sweet dream came to a quick conclusion. We left the cow shed invigorated. We began to march briskly after a good rest and were surprisingly not hungry. The train was waiting, the locomotive hissing impatiently, sending a volley of sparks into the wintery sky. We jumped quickly into the cattle cars.

I held the potatoes firmly, a sweet reward of the day. Who knew if I would ever again encounter this divine stroke of luck. My life was rapidly approaching the limits of human endurance, there was nothing more to look for, to hope for.

The train came to a sudden halt, the wheels screeching continuously, the locomotive releasing steam with a prolonged hiss. We jumped out of the train onto soft snowy ground. Another day was gone in our short life span.

The SS colony was peaceful, shrouded in a heavy snow blanket. The little houses looked like those from a children's storybook, the lights glowing in the windows. The springy German music sounded quietly in the winter night. We passed the main gate—"*Mutze ab,*" the recurrent tribute, "*Morituri te salutant*" (the dead greet you).

I quickly passed the gate dividing the big camp from the small one. Berek was waiting outside the barracks. He seemed worried but relieved when he saw me.

"I was worried," he said. He was haggard, emaciated.

"It took more time than usual, the guards were invited by a German farmer for hot coffee. Bolek, look what I've got," I said proudly. "Guess what?"

"I don't know, I don't believe in surprises anymore," he said sadly.

"I'll give you a clue, it's round."

"I know—potatoes."

"You're right; I won a prize for excellent performance."

"What performance?" Berek asked curiously.

"I knocked down a couple of concrete blocks in the Reichsbank. Nobody else could do it."

Berek didn't ask more questions.

"Five potatoes for me, five for you," I said dividing the potatoes equally. We went to our bunks. The potatoes were cold, icy. "What do you think Bolek?"

Berek was two years older than me. He lifted his eyes. "I think one potato per day," Berek said.

"I think you are right," I answered, wrapping the potatoes in the newspaper.

One potato per day.

13

SPRING

MARCH BROUGHT a spell of warm weather. Water was dripping from the barracks roof. The blast of chill wind brought the fragrance of awakening nature. Spring was coming. Was she? Spring in Buchenwald? Was it possible, Spring in a domain ruled by Evil?

Fabian Gershon was the BBC of Block 62. Nobody knew how he knew, but he knew. One day he brought the big news. The news was encouraging: Germany was losing the war. The American forces had taken Achen. The war had finally come to German soil.

In Weimar, traces of war were visible. The Germans were carrying bundles, pushing carts, despondent, sensing the approaching demise of the Third Reich. The maniacal idea of a demented outcast brought to the Germans unprecedented misery. The same Germans who in a frenzy glorified their leader were digging in the rubble of their dreams. The German Empire was crumbling.

The roll call got off on the wrong foot. Two inmates were missing. The search was meticulous, but to no avail. Usually the missing were the dead ones, but no dead could be found. *Musulmans* didn't try to escape, they could hardly walk.

Stanko went berserk. No shortage was allowed. The body

count was of paramount importance. Vasil tried to help, he searched the bunks but with no luck. Finally he entered the latrines in a desperate effort to solve the enigma. He was doing it for the third time, but now he took his time. Soon he reappeared smiling.

"*Naszol, naszol, skurwej syny upaly w Jamu* (I found them—these two bastards fell into the shit pit)." This was the case. The two missing inmates had drowned in the excrement pit. Two striped inmates caps were floating on top of the pool. The SS officer was called to verify the *corpus delicti*. He did it reluctantly.

After the body count something unusual happened. Before leaving, the SS officer handed Stanko a sheet of paper. Stanko began to call off numbers.

"*Haftling* (inmate) 1 1 5 7 1 3."

I froze, my heart pounding. I looked at my number again. Yes, this was my number. The last two numbers were 13. Berek turned pale. There were more numbers called off, but not too many. Berek's number wasn't called; it meant separation. I stared at my brother, tears in my eyes. We were so close to each other. Berek was my father, my mother. He gave me moral support. He always used to say, "We will make it." Now he was fading away, his body fragile, emaciated, devastated by the ravages of starvation. We would not share the end together. I was physically stronger than Berek.

"All the numbers which I called off will be transfered immediately to Block 47 in the big camp," Stanko announced in terse voice. The numbers called off were of those inmates belonging to the Weimar group.

"Bolek?"

"Yes."

"I feel guilty," I said fighting back my tears.

"Don't be silly, you are not the one to make the judgment."

"Bolek, will we survive?"

"I hope. We bear a message, the last two of the entire Bender and Szylit families."

"You mean to say that our parents are dead?"

"Yes, I am afraid so, you know better than me, they hid in the bunker for several weeks. I wish I could believe in miracles."

"Bolek, remember, if we survive, wait at the main gate."

We embraced, crying, failing to find words of consolation. We were helpless, rejected, and now separated. I took my blanket, spoon, tin plate. Tears covered my face. The departure resembled a funeral. I had the feeling that I would never see him again. I began to walk, waving my hand. Berek stood in the barrack door waving too. I passed the gate between the small and the big camp. I stared back. Berek was still waving, then he disappeared.

Block 47 in the big camp was quite different from Block 62 in the small camp. No beatings, no Stanko, the bunks weren't congealed. The slice of bread somehow thicker. The soup less watery.

I continued to work at Weimar but the work got harder. My strength was diminishing day by day. The loneliness was unbearable. I was heartbroken. Berek was always on my mind. I was getting sick too. My body was shaking violently in spells of recurring fever. I couldn't swallow. My inflamed throat was in pain. The slice of bread which I couldn't eat was stolen by my neighbor. This was my fault. The safest deposit box was the stomach.

To be sick in Buchenwald was tantamount to death. Sick people were eliminated by the injection of carbolic acid into the heart; death was instantaneous. With my immune system collapsed, the gate was wide open to any calamity. I shuffled my feet like an old man.

One morning I made up my mind. I left the barracks and headed for the *Revir* (the hospital). The *Revir* was for the political inmates only. This was my last chance, if there was any, to get medical help. I was mentally prepared for the last encounter, because my present situation meant death anyway. I had lost my will power.

The *Revir* consisted of several barracks, surrounded by flowers. I was surprised to see flowers in Buchenwald. Nature doesn't discriminate. The soil in this hostile place was probably the same as in other places. Only the cruelty of men depriving others of food, clothing, and shelter makes nature harsh and inhumane.

It was now the beginning of April. Spring was in the air. The rays of sun penetrated the clouds, briefly embracing the frozen bodies longing for a warm touch. Birds were chirping, bringing a message of life even to a place ruled by the disciples of Heinrich Himmler. The air was still chilly, but a far cry from the Arctic winds of January.

Would I get medical help? Healthy men were dying; why should the Germans help the sick? The *Revir* was located on a steep hill. The ascent gave me heart palpitations. A large group of inmates stood next to the hospital door waiting for the doctor. The average age of the sick inmates was between twenty-five and thirty-five. No question that I was the youngest, but this was meaningless. They gave me a hostile look, having the notion that every additional patient would diminish their chances of reception.

We didn't wait too long. A doctor in a white uniform appeared in the door. He was medium height, in his thirties, short-cut receding hair, brown eyes. On his left arm he had an arm band with an inscription *Arzt* (doctor).

"There will be no reception today," he said in a terse voice. He turned back to enter the hospital barracks, then he stopped and turned back. "*Du*, step out." Several inmates, still standing, rushed to the front. "Not you, idiots, the young fellow at the rear," the doctor shouted angrily.

I pointed at myself in disbelief.

"Yes, you," said the doctor.

I stepped forward, losing my balance; I felt dizzy and nauseous. The doctor helped me to enter the room. "Wait here," he said, "I will be back in a few minutes."

He disappeared, leaving me alone. I gazed around. The room was small, probably the entrance to the doctor's office. Before me was an oblong mirror. I looked into the mirror, then I looked back, to see who was standing behind me. I didn't recognize myself. It wasn't me—the mirror held a reflection of death. I had turned into a skeleton, nothing resembling a human creature. Since the departure from Hasag I hadn't had a chance to look at myself. When I saw the external features of other inmates, I never could visualize that I was already one of them.

The doctor came back. "Are you a Jew?" he asked. He asked in German.

"Yes I am a Jew."

"Where do you come from?"

"Czestochowa, Poland."

The doctors eyes lit up. "You can speak to me in Polish," he said calmly and reassuringly. "How old are you?"

"If today is April 5, I am seventeen," I said, breathing heavily.

"You are quite lucky, today is April 5," the doctor said smiling. "I happened to dislike Jews, but when I saw you, you brought back memories. I have a brother your age, there's a striking resemblance between the two of you. You are in very bad shape. I will try to help you. It's quite complicated. I am putting myself in jeopardy. I already spoke to the main French doctor. From now on you are not a Jew. I see you speak German fluently."

"Yes," I answered relieved.

"Let me take your temperature, then take a shower, you are filthy," he said, putting a thermometer under my arm. After a couple of minutes he took it out. "Well, you are running a high temperature, a severe case of influenza, maybe even pleurisy. In this condition you wouldn't last for too long," the doctor said, giving me an injection. "I have to leave," he said, handing me a towel and a long white tunic. "After you finish, Dyck will take care of you. He is Dutch, don't be afraid, he knows that you are a Jew," the doctor added, leaving the room. He disappeared like a phantom.

I was in the Buchenwald hospital on my birthday, just a short walk from the small camp. This wasn't a dream, but reality. I didn't believe in miracles, but the encounter with the doctor was beyond comprehension. In a matter of minutes I had moved up to the level of a human being. I hadn't seen a towel for years. We had been using rags. Before I took a shower, with faucets on the inside, I used the toilet. To sit on a toilet seat was painful, I didn't have buttocks. Toilet tissue was a rarity, even newspaper wasn't always available. I entered a world of fantasy. I was thrilled to rediscover the basic little things which brought back sweet memories of home. If I could only share this precious moment with my brother.

The shower was balming, invigorating, the first after three months of my incarceration in Buchenwald. I was able to adjust the water temperature. The soap had a mild fragrance. Blood was gently throbbing in my veins. I could have stayed under the shower for hours, but I shut off the faucet because of dizzy spells. After drying my body with the towel, I put on the white tunic. I looked at myself and began to giggle. I resembled a church choir boy.

Dyck entered the shower room. He was over six foot tall, with crew cut hair, brown eyes, a round face, and a big warm smile. A radiant human smile I hadn't encountered for years.

"My name is Dyck," he introduced himself. "You will be under my care, and care you need. There are no Jews in this hospital except you. If somebody asks you about religion, be aware of it."

"Yes I understand," I said, my voice inaudible. My heart was beating in my ears. I felt that my whole system was on the verge of collapsing.

Dyck lifted me. "You are light like a feather," he said carrying me effortlessly. We entered a huge room similar in shape to an army barrack. Long rows of beds with patients on each side of the room. The bloodless faces of the patients were reminiscent of wax figures. The beds were snow white. "I will be back soon," Dyck said, covering me with a blanket.

The sudden change was beyond the realm of reality. I thought I was hallucinating. Since my departure from Garibaldi Street 18, where I lived with my parents for a short time, I hadn't enjoyed a clean white bed. I had left Garibaldi Street in the summer of 1943. In Hasag there were no beds, only wooden bunks with coarse burlap straw mattresses. Dyck came back with a bowl of steaming soup.

"Eat slowly, the soup is hot, but you will enjoy it." He put the tray on my lap.

I stared at the steaming bowl in disbelief. Milk and noodles, thick round noodles, glistening, beautifully shaped. I didn't know how to start, how to eat, noodle by noodle, to prolong the joy of eating. I tasted cautiously. The taste was divine, sheer ecstasy, the noodles gentle, sweet to the palate. I ate slowly, breathing heavily. The sharp pain in my chest didn't diminish. I leaned back on the pillow. I had difficulties swallowing, or my stomach was unable to receive the food. After a rest I continued to eat slowly—under no circumstance would I leave this soup unfinished.

Dyck reappeared in the door. "How do you feel?" he asked softly, taking the tray.

"I feel great, but dizzy and weak. There is also a nagging feeling that this dream will not last for too long."

"Don't be a fool," Dyck said reassuringly, "the Americans are very close to Weimar, the day of liberation is at hand."

"Dyck, are you really telling me the truth, or are you just trying to make me feel better?"

"Look, the Americans took Jena and Fulda. It won't be too long before they're here. Now take a rest, a good sleep, forget that you are in Buchenwald."

I grabbed Dyck's hand and pressed it to my lips, tears in my eyes. Dyck caressed my hand and placed it gently under the blanket. "I'll see you tomorrow," he said leaving the room.

My mind was numb, I tried to reconstruct the last day's happenings to no avail. No Stanko any more, no more deadly roll calls, or Vasil chasing the inmates into the latrines. My thoughts were with my brother. What was he doing now?

On my birthday I got a gift of life. I hadn't done anything to enhance my chances for survival. I sailed aimlessly on the rough sea, pushed violently by the winds of fate. No effort on my part to change the course of my life. Who was in charge? Was it the Master of the Universe? The same One indifferent to the sufferings of millions? Was it the same One unmoved by the cries of babies thrown like wood logs into the furnaces of Auschwitz and Treblinka? Was it only a blind fate? I will never know the answer. Where was Berek now? He was cold, hungry, deserted. I felt a burning feeling of guilt for being in the hospital. I fell asleep.

The morning sun came through the window, planting a beam of light on the floor. I woke up. My eyelids were heavy. I couldn't bring my thoughts together. Everything was rushing like a stormy river. I was disoriented, trying to recapture the previous day.

"Good morning." Dyck entered the room greeting me with a smile. He was carrying a tray. This time milk with rice. It was inconceivable how all these goodies were still available in Buchenwald.

"Dyck, tell me, who is the generous donor?" I asked curiously.

"Medicine, as well food provisions, are sent by the Swiss Red Cross," Dyck replied. "As a matter of fact, certain inmates in the big camp get packages from the Red Cross."

Our conversation was disrupted by two doctors who entered the room speaking French.

"Jurek," Dyck said before leaving the room. "You will undergo certain tests, nothing serious."

One of the doctors held in his hand an oversized injection device. The needle was very long. The doctor ordered me to leave the bed. I lifted my tunic exposing my back. The doctor firmly pulled the tunic over my head, locking my hands. In a swift movement he thrust the needle into my lung. I bit my lip, writhing in pain. The test was quick. The doctors left without saying a word.

Dyck helped me back into bed. "Don't worry, you're okay, the pain will pass. The most important thing is that there are no traces of water," Dyck said reassuringly.

I closed my eyes. My body was fluttering. The punctured lung was emanating waves of burning pain. Darkness was creeping again in the corners of the hospital room. A small red bulb at the entrance was glowing dimly. The thuds of artillery explosions came from far away. The ground trembled in expectation of the approaching liberation. The sky flashed intermittently with crisscross beams of search lights. The piercing pain receded. I fell asleep.

The change in my physical condition was unprecedented, taking in account that this sanitarium was Buchenwald and not Davos. Dyck fed me constantly, in conspiracy. One day for breakfast he brought me two thick slices of bread with margarine, topped off with fruit jam and a glass of hot milk. "You are improving miraculously," Dyck said, visibly happy.

"Thanks to you. I never had a chance," I answered.

"Jurek, there are visible signs that something is brewing in the camp," Dyck said immersed in thoughts. "The SS personnel are running madly, but they are still in firm command. There are persistent rumors that the Germans intend to evacuate Buchenwald and erase the camp. They are getting jittery about leaving the *corpus delicti* behind them. I hope they don't have time to do it. In the event somebody comes to the hospital and asks you to move, stay in bed, don't dare move. *Verstanden?*" Dyck concluded jokingly.

"*Jawohl,*" I said smiling.

"I will be back in a couple hours, or maybe even before. I will snoop around to get some more information," Dyck said leaving the room.

A roar of an airplane engine broke the silence, accompanied by a short burst of a machine gun. The plane was flying low. I leaned on my elbow to get a better view through the window opposite my bed.

The roll call square, the *Appell-Platz*, usually deserted during the day, was patrolled by SS units. The loudspeaker came alive in short barking orders. "*Achtung, Achtung, samtliche Juden ans Tor* (every Jew to the main gate)." The Jews were still on the Germans' mind, even in moments of approaching defeat. In a matter of minutes the square filled with people. The inmates approached the square from all different points, their bodies shrouded in blankets. Surely Berek was among them.

Dyck came rushing into the room, visibly agitated. "Jurek,

this is it. The Germans are evacuating Buchenwald. The first to go are the Jews, Gypsies and the Russian officers from the big camp. This is the first priority."

"Dyck what day is today?"

"April 10."

"I am thinking about my brother."

"Jurek, I am sorry, I understand your feelings, but there is nothing we can do about this."

"Dyck, look, I can't believe it," I said pointing towards the main gate.

The roll call square was humming like a beehive. The sight was unreal. Inmates lay on the ground covered with blankets. The SS soldiers were kicking the motionless bodies which refused to walk. Sporadic shots were fired.

The thud of artillery explosions shook the windows. The story of the not too distant past was unfolding again. Only three months before, in the evacuation of Hasag, with the Russians fighting the Germans at the outskirts of Czestochowa, at the last moment the Germans took the Jews with them. Now Americans were fighting the Germans at the outskirts of Weimar. Again the last minute tragedy. The Jews would not be allowed to see the dawn of liberation. The hell of Buchenwald had one exit only. The German bestiality was being played out to the very end.

The emaciated inmates couldn't even walk a few yards, how could they walk miles? The sinister idea of evacuation was meant to eliminate the Jews in a last orgy of German fury. Dyck was visibly upset by the gruesome evacuation sight. I was devastated. Where was Berek now? Was he alive? Was it possible he could walk? Dyck left the room.

The scenes of forced evacuation continued for hours. The recalcitrant inmates were dragged one by one to join the marching columns on their last march. Some corpses lay motionless, shrouded with their blankets, at last celebrating their ultimate freedom, redeemed by sudden death. I closed my eyes, I was shaking uncontrollably.

In the early hours of the next day, Dyck came flying into the room and he almost stumbled. "Jurek, it is over, they are here, I am telling you, they are here!"

"Dyck, I don't understand, who is here?"

"The Americans are here!"

"Did you see them?" I asked in disbelief.

"Yes, I saw them with my eyes, the first tanks arrived just minutes ago. What a splendid sight. No Krauts anymore!"

Dyck was swirling around, shouting in ecstasy, "Free, free forever, I am going home." He stopped abruptly and said apologetically, "Jurek, please forgive my outpourings, I know your case is different, but you will be all right. Today on liberation day I will serve you a good meal, tomorrow you are on your own. You were supposed to be discharged today, excellent timing! Your clothes are in the storage room." Dyck embraced me firmly, "Goodbye, who knows, maybe our paths will cross again."

I stood up, feeling weak. I stared at the beds around me. Motionless people, wax masks, totally unaware that finally they were free. I wanted to scream, to share with them the moment of joy, but I couldn't. There was no joy in my heart, but a gaping emptiness. I stepped forward to the window. Berek was supposed to wait at the main gate.

Where was the enigmatic Polish doctor, whom I hadn't seen

since I entered the hospital? He had saved my life on the spur of the moment. He had turned back to pick me, the only one from the entire group. I wanted to thank him.

I went back to my bed, my mind numb. I was reluctant to leave the hospital, my home, my salvation. I wanted to cry, but I couldn't. My mind was hollow, deactivated, at a loss to understand the substance of the newly acquired freedom. I was afraid to walk out to face the new alien world. Would I ever be able to regain my lost human dignity all alone? Here, in the hospital, like a rejected dog, I had found shelter. I was afraid to walk to the gate, or to the barracks, to face the ultimate truth. I was afraid that the reality outside would destroy my illusion.

Dyck came in with a steaming bowl of soup, and a lot of bread. "Look what I brought you today, potatoes and meat, enjoy it. After a week of a dairy diet you are allowed to have meat. I just hope the inmates will avoid meat, it'll make them sick."

"Dyck, goodbye," I embraced him warmly. "For the rest of my life I will never forget. I will miss you. You gave me the feeling of being a human being, the first human touch I encountered since I left home."

"Jurek, listen," Dyck said visibly moved. "This is a great beginning for all of us, we are joining the family of mankind again. Be strong, you are young, and you seem to be a smart boy, you are sensitive and gentle, you will be well accepted anywhere, you will go back to school and in years to come you will establish a family," Dyck concluded, tears in his eyes. He was gently stroking my prickly hair. We looked at each other for the last time. Dyck left the room.

I began to sob. I was on my own, no link to the past, lost in the universe, not knowing to whom to turn. I walked into the storage room. Nobody was inside. My clothes were on the front shelf with my inmate number in front of them. I decided not to take my old clothes. I tore off my inmate number. I picked the best clothes, best shoes, a jacket, a blue shirt, a pair of socks, even a belt, a rarity in Buchenwald. I left the hospital room and headed for the main gate, the promised meeting point with Berek. It was around eleven in the morning.

For the first time since I had arrived in Buchenwald, I took a good look at the notorious big camp. How different the big camp was from the small camp. The place looked like a battlefield, total chaos. I saw Germans retreating in disarray on horses, bicycles, on foot. I saw SS caught and thrown alive into the excrement pits, their SS hats with the dead scull emblem floating on the surface. The guards were leaving their posts, changing their uniforms into civilian clothes. I didn't pay any attention to them, my mind was on my brother.

The ground adjacent to the gatehouse was covered with bodies. Many had torn blankets over their heads. These inmates had refused to join the final death march to Dachau; some were wounded, some were dead. The scene was gruesome. The gate was deserted except for some American soldiers stationed outside the gate at the German colony previously occupied by the SS. At the side of the road jeeps and half tracks were parked. I stood ten or fifteen yards from the main gate. The huge roll call square was full of American soldiers, General Patton's best, tall black men, six footers, with colorful scarves around their necks. I had never seen black men before. They were unreal to me. The soldiers were trying to help, carrying inmates on stretchers, some dead, some dying and stretching out their hands and saying, "Brother, I'm dying, give me your hand."

The soldiers were in shock, crying like babies. They gave them their hands. Some inmates were just sitting, stupified.

I accelerated my walk, the gate was in sight. Some black soldiers were peeling oranges—I hadn't seen an orange since 1939. The sound of the English language brought me warm memories of when I would catch a few words in English from my brother then studying English in high school. I fixed my eyes on the trees. The trees were filled with cherry blossoms. Gorgeous white flowers, reminiscent of brides walking to the wedding altar. This was a splendid manifestation of life. For some it was a belated message.

The road was a windy one, and on both sides were small picturesque houses, manicured grass and islets of flowers. I had seen those houses in winter covered with snow on my way back from Weimar where I was cleaning rubble. The former habitat of the SS. I was surprised to see children's swings in the backyard of the houses. Life didn't stop in Buchenwald. Here the SS families maintained a serene life style. How had the German children viewed us?

I was alone. The main gate was deserted. Berek wasn't there as promised. Perhaps he was evacuated with many others. I turned on my way back to the small camp, Block 62 and 55. Nobody was there. Some inmates were walking in a daze, half insane. I stared at each one. I checked the bunks, hoping to find Berek there. I stood for a while undecided, not knowing what to do next. Suddenly I saw a familiar face, Fabian Gershon. He was carrying a small pail of soup, full to the brim.

"Jurek!" exalted Fabian joyously, "you look wonderful!"

I didn't pay attention to his compliment, Berek was on my mind. "Where are all the Hasag people?"

"Nobody here," Fabian answered, preoccupied with his soup.

"Fabian, do you mean to say that they marched them out?"

"Yes, they took all of them, including Bolek."

"Do you have any information about their fate?" I asked, my heart pounding uncontrollably.

"Jurek, I am sorry to say, but there are no hopes, no one could walk. How could they march to Dachau for God's sake?"

I didn't ask questions anymore. This was the end of the saga of the Benders. I was the last.

Fabian was purring like a cat, searching with his spoon for pieces of meat. He had always been obsessed with how dense the soup was. Even during the years in Hasag Fabian bragged about the density of his soup. Intentionally he waited to be the last in the line, until the soup kettle reached the lowest level. His patience and determination always paid off. Fabian Gershon had come to Czestochowa from Lodz. His parents and his sister had been sent to Treblinka.

"Don't you want to know how I succeeded in fooling the German bastards?" Fabian asked bitterly.

"Fabian I am really sorry but I was thinking about my brother," I said apologetically.

"From the Hasag group there are three known survivors," he began. "You, myself and Itzhak Rosenblum. I decided not to go. I crawled under a heap of dead bodies, it wasn't hard. I played dead. I left enough room to breathe. I knew that the Americans were only few miles away. I took a chance. I was willing to die but not to repeat the mistake of Hasag. I am sorry for Bolek, he hid himself, but he left his hideout after being offered a loaf of bread. This was sheer deception, the Germans never gave bread to the evacuees. I am really sorry. He was your brother but he was also my good friend," he concluded.

There was a depressing silence.

Fabian was preoccupied with his soup. "Excellent soup, a lot of meat and potatoes, American style. I love those Americans, easygoing, informal, they treat you like a human being. By the way, Itzhak Rosenblum is in the hospital with pleurisy. If you want to see him, we can go tomorrow to the hospital. We'll get him some soup, a lift of vitality. I am sure he will be glad to see us."

"Another thing," he added, "don't forget to register at the UNRRA (United Nations Relief and Rehabilitation Administration) office, at the main gate. The UNRRA is enabling the displaced to return to their mother countries. I would never go back to Poland. Poland is a big cemetery for all Jews. I prefer the USA or Switzerland, or the last resort, Palestine. I personally prefer Switzerland, a dream country, no wars, a lot of cows, milk, cheese, butter and good chocolate. I want to study, to be somebody, to have some purpose in life. Life will go on. Finally, after the stomach ecstasy, we will have to put our lives together. I think that the very sick will be allowed to settle in Switzerland. Probably the ones with tuberculosis will go to Davos, Switzerland," Fabian concluded. "Okay, Jurek, I'll see you tomorrow, I am going to secure some more food…the war is over, but you never know."

I stood for a while. I was all by myself, no brother to care for, no one to turn to, no one to talk to. This wasn't the kind of liberation I expected. The sudden trauma of the "new reality," was excruciating and unbearable.

I went to UNRRA located in one of the barracks, near the

main gate. I was interviewed by a woman, an official of the UNRRA. She was Swiss, in her thirties, blond, blue eyes, her hair pulled together at the back of her head in a braided knot. She looked very German, efficient, dry, very formal, no smile, dressed in a bluish grey army uniform.

"Are you feeling okay?" she asked in a brusque voice, staring straight into my eyes.

I felt uncomfortable in her presence. There was something German in her behavior and appearance. "I feel okay. I was just discharged from the hospital."

"So you were in a hospital?" she repeated in disbelief.

I wasn't ready to go into a detailed explanation. The International Red Cross, sending packages to Buchenwald, was inclined to believe in the Potemkin services in the big camp. Food packages never arrived in the small camp.

"I will need some information from you," the Swiss official began. "You will undergo a medical check up. If everything is okay, you will be sent with a group of orphans to France, under the auspices of UNRRA. You will recuperate in a transit camp, in Metz, Alsace Lorraine." She spoke in a soldiery manner. No mention about school, education, nothing, just a transit camp.

"Will I stay in France?" I asked shyly.

"No, the French are repatriating their own people. They are not interested in an influx of other refugees. From Metz you will go to Marseille on your way to Palestine, where you will join a group of youngsters in a kibbutz. Good luck." she said.

I left her office without a word, deeply disappointed. I went to the barracks confused and depressed. The idea of going to

Palestine didn't appeal to me. I wanted to study medicine. In Palestine I would be a farmer.

Why did I want to be a doctor? I wanted to help other needy people, like the English doctor-writer, Cronin, who helped poor coal miners without accepting an honorarium. In Palestine I would join a kibbutz and be a farmer for the rest of my life. I didn't want that, but I didn't have a choice. I was an orphan, a nobody, the last of an extinct generation.

But still, Palestine was close to my heart. No more stigma of humiliation, the eternal image of the damned Jew. I would find my way among my own people. My uncle, the brother of my father, was living in Palestine. He had left Poland in 1939, two months before the outbreak of World War II. There was another second cousin, a high ranking officer in the British police corps. But would I be able to establish a family? Was it possible out of the consumed embers to retrieve a complete log of wood?

The next day I took a train to Weimar. This time not a cattle train, but a passenger train, ticket free. The German conductor was amiable. I didn't question his past record, because German cattle trains were operated without conductors. Germany was going through a drastic change, with the Third Reich lying in ruins. Arrogance was gone, giving vent to subdued meekness. When the conductor asked me for ticket, I answered proudly, "I am *ein ehemalige Haftling* (a former inmate)." This was an awesome and magic word, no further explanations were required. Free ride, all paid by the vanquished Germany. Even on the last ride to Auschwitz and Treblinka the condemned Jews were charged for the fateful trip, the fees credited to the Reichsbank, paid out of the victims' stolen property.

After the liberation of Buchenwald, the Germans of Weimar swarmed to the camps en masse to witness the horrors of their insane leadership. Just in crushing defeat, the Germans came to sudden realization and awareness, claiming in shock a lack of information and deception. "We didn't know," some were crying in a sudden surge of emotions. They couldn't believe that these horrors were conducted next to their doors. Now they were traveling to Buchenwald back and forth, visiting a strange zoo, or a museum of an extinct human tribe. The picture they saw brought them many sleepless nights.

On the train I met a German girl, a teenager, long blond hair, blue eyes. She was first to introduce herself. "I am Rita Muller," she said politely.

I nodded my head, reluctant to talk.

"Are you from the camp?" She avoided mentioning the word Buchenwald.

"Yes I am from the camp," I answered nonchalantly.

"Is it true what we are being told about the Nazi atrocities?" She wanted first hand information.

"What you were told before by Adolf Hitler, your leader, was a lie, what you heard and saw now is true. The *Musulmans* you saw used to be normal human beings," I answered icily.

She was pale, speechless.

"How old are you?" I asked, struggling to control my ire. My words came out rapidly. I didn't want to wait for a single answer. "What was your father doing during the war?" I continued.

"I am seventeen, my father was killed in Stalingrad, he was serving in the Wermacht," she answered defensively.

I didn't know whether to believe her. Every good German

died in Stalingrad. At the "battle fields" of Treblinka and Auschwitz the Germans didn't die. I looked straight into her eyes. She challenged my look. She wasn't lying.

"What about you?" I continued to press. "I am sure you served in *Hitlerjugend*."

"Yes, I was, I am not denying it, but I was in school. I didn't have a choice. In school we were obliged to undergo paramilitary service. I couldn't say no. They would punish me and throw me out of the school. At home my parents never taught me to hate, the hate came from outside. My father knew that the dream of a thousand year Third Reich would come to a bitter end. He was a soldier on the eastern front," she concluded in a firm voice.

"How can I believe you?" I said angrily. "I was working in Weimar, emaciated, starved to death. Your people were so aloof, indifferent. In the eyes of the Germans we were the *Untermensche*, the damned slaves of the *Herrenvolk*. What makes people superior or inferior? We are born the same way and we die the same way. God doesn't discriminate, but the problem was that you didn't believe in God, you wanted to test him and you won, because the ruthless power rested with you," I concluded agitated.

She looked at me disoriented, defenseless. "I am not trying to defend Germany. Our guilt is collective, for knowing or not knowing. The people who inflicted on you this cruel sufferings were Germans. The gas chambers were German made. The idea of the final solution was German. You might not believe me, but I am ashamed to be German, because the stain on our conscience will remain for ages. Decent Germans could refuse the orders to kill, nothing would happen to them, the only

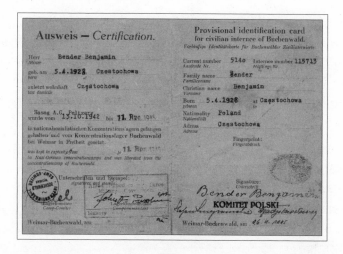

Identification card provided to Benjamin on the day of his liberation from incarceration at Buchenwald, April 11, 1945.

punishment was to be sent to the Eastern front. They didn't do it because they were cowards. In no way can you forgive us. There is no way we can repent for the atrocities we have committed," she said, tears streaming down her face.

The train came to a screeching halt. She stretched out her hand, subdued, despondent. I looked at her, not knowing what to do next. She saw me hesitating but she kept her hand stretched out. I squeezed her hand, speechless, at a loss to utter a word. The Germans destroyed everything I had, my parents, grandparents and finally my only brother at the dawn of liberation. I couldn't look into her eyes, feeling that I committed blasphemy by betraying the sacred memory of my family. She was sobbing. When we parted she kept waving her hand.

I was furious, boiling inside, at a loss to understand the Ger-

man psyche. All babies have the same beautiful smile, regardless of religion; Jewish babies and German babies couldn't hate
each other. Why would they under Hitler? What was required
for a German to reach the plateau of abysmal bestiality? How
does it work?

I walked aimlessly, gazing at the Germans. I was overwhelmed with fleeting joy. The Germans, once proud, arro-
gant, aloof, now beaten and defeated. Houses in ruins. Dreams
in ruins. Future in ruins. People in despair pushing wheeled
carts with their belongings, but still better off than the Jews
waiting naked and horrified before the entrance to the gas
chambers.

I passed the Goethe monument once again. I walked in a
daze trying to reconstruct the moments of anguish, death,
humiliation, inflicted on the Jews by their former masters. I
didn't realize it, but I was walking on a bridge. Someone was
honking impatiently. I was blocking traffic. I turned sharply
to the right. I remembered this bridge from the Allied air attacks, when I had once taken cover underneath. The German
SS guards had been scared to death, aiming their rifles at the
attacking planes. At those moments I prayed to God to be killed
by a bomb. Miracles didn't happen.

I bent over the bridge rail. The water was murky, stained
with big oil rings, tinted with rainbow colors. For a moment
I thought of putting an end to my life. My parents had done
the same thing. The threads with the past were torn, nobody
would bemoan me, nobody would utter a word of regret. To
begin a life on a heap of ashes seemed utterly grotesque. Can
a human being survive in the absence of love and friendship?

I was the last of a large family, left to carry the pain of the nightmare the rest of my life. I had to live to tell the story to my future family, to be a grandfather with a lot of grandchildren. To destroy myself was foolish, to accomplish what the Germans couldn't accomplish. The idea was senseless and utterly preposterous. The hour was getting late. I wanted to run away from this cursed soil, bearing the bones of my brother, whom I loved and respected. His grave was unknown, like many others.

———

The continuous explosions and distant drone of aircraft were getting closer. The battlefront had come to Buchenwald.

"Achtung, Achtung, samtliche Juden ans Tor (all the Jews to the main gate)."

The message came through the loudspeaker, being repeated again and again. Block 55, the block for the youngsters, was deserted. Berek lifted his emaciated body with difficulty. He could hardly move, feeling his life melting away. The bunks around him were empty. His mind ceased to function, everything was blurred. Only a week before, Benjamin, stricken with a high fever, left Block 62 in a daze. Berek was then transferred to Block 55. Benjamin had gone to get medical help. He never came back. Was he still alive? Buchenwald had no medical care. The Revir was only for the privileged, but not for the Jews. He had seen his brother for the last time crossing the small gate on his way to the big camp.

The barrack was supervised by Gustaf, a German communist, red haired, a good decent human being, willing to help. Gustaf tried to bring some joy to the hearts of the youngsters. During the winter evenings poetry was recited on Gustaf's initiative. Berek recited Julian Tuvim's The Locomotive. *Only the day before, the group of youngsters, on their way to the barrack, was stopped and marched out. That day Berek hadn't left the barrack with the rest. He hadn't had food for two days. The Germans wanted the inmates out of their barracks. The most effective way was to deprive them of the meager ration of bread.*

The footsteps outside the barrack got closer. Berek squeezed his frail body into the dugout, covering himself with wooden boards. He was lying on his belly, his parched lips touching the moist soil. Someone entered the barrack. Berek's heart was pounding.

"Leave your hideouts. The small camp is mined. If you leave voluntarily, nothing will happen to you. A loaf of bread will be given to everyone."

The words were in Polish, Berek's hopes rose at once. He left his dugout and was momentarily blinded by the daylight. A powerful blow made him realize his mistake. It was too late.

"Los, los!"

Another hit and another. The Lagerschutz kicked him repeatedly with his nailed boot. Outside the barrack Berek joined a group of inmates, probably, like him, caught by the deceitful promise of bread. No bread was given. The Germans were masters of deceit. The Jews entering the gas chambers were given soap and towels. The promise of survival bordered on irrationality.

The big camp was swarming with SS. Inmates were lying on the ground covered with blankets, refusing to move. The SS were literally walking on the bodies trying in vain to lift the refusing inmates to a standing position. The eerie scene was beyond human grasp. Hundreds of bodies, skeletons, half alive, refusing German orders for the first time. The commandant was mad. He couldn't believe his eyes. Precious time was being wasted because of these stinking bastards. He called for reinforcements, giving orders to shoot, even to drench them with kerosene, to turn them to blazing torches. His orders went into effect immediately.

The dignified Musulmans' *resistance couldn't match the fire power of the SS. One by one, the inmates were dragged, some pulled by hands and legs. The march was already in progress. Some faces were familiar to Berek, faces of friends from Hasag, now extinguished, their bodies emaciated, bearing the stigma of death. During the three months in Buchenwald, they had lost the external human appearance. Three months ago they had left Czestochowa strong, full of life. They had hopes while marching to the waiting trains in orderly fashion. They were fooled by hope. Now they were dehumanized, a pack of rustling bones, covered with yellow decaying skin, sunken eyes, protruding hips. The marchers were being pushed to the side of the road by the escorting SS guards freeing the road for the cars, trucks and horses.*

The surrounding hills were still covered with snow, although the smell of spring was permeating the air. The ground was slippery. A sudden fall meant death. The SS guards were nervous and impatient. Some inmates lost their shoes, their wounded feet bleeding. The scene was horrifying, rows of inmates moving in a long cortege, participating in their own funeral. Occasionally shots were fired but nobody dared to turn his head. The weak, not able to walk, were executed instantly.

An inmate walking next to Berek began to weep, whispering his mother's name. He stopped walking, and he stood in a state of torpor, crying like a lost baby. The escorting SS guard jumped out of the side road. A shot was fired point blank, reverberating in the mountains. The inmate fell face down. For him the struggle was over. A victory in defeat. The long hand of the Third Reich could not reach him anymore.

After a few hours, the exhausted marchers approached a forest glade surrounded by tall trees. "Fifteen minutes rest," shouted the guards.

The inmates collapsed on the ground. Some fell prostrate, hardly showing a sign of life. Some crouched, wrapped in their blankets. The ground was still wet. Berek sat on a wide rugged stone protruding from the ground. He pulled the blanket over his head, then leaning his head on his knees, he fell asleep instantly.

The commanding SS officers gave orders to the guards to take up positions. Some began promptly to reload their rifles. Some trucks moved closer to the forest. The SS soldiers inside the trucks lifted the green canvas covering. The mounted Spandau machine guns were directed towards the resting inmates. Time came to a standstill.

A screamed order. "Fire!"

The clatter of machine guns. Some of the SS threw grenades. Screams of dying, cut off prayers of "Shma Israel!" uttered in the last moments of agony. Last words cast towards the mute sky by people betrayed by God. The mass execution proceeded smoothly, efficient to the best of German ability. Some of the inmates tried to escape the ring of fire, but to no avail. They were caught and thrown by the impact of the bullets. Some died in their slumber, not witnessing the gruesome moments of their death. At last, the tormented found redemption.

The rattle of the machine guns continued, turning the forest glade into a blazing inferno. The ground was littered with bodies, grotesque, broken rag dolls. Then the shooting abruptly came to a halt. No voices, no sounds, only the rustle of the tree branches moved by a gentle April breeze. The SS left their positions to check the dead bodies. Sporadic shots were still being heard to finish off the half alive. From the Hasag group only one survived this death march, Mietek Kongrecki, who was from Czestochowa. Before the inmates reached the forest glade he had hurled his body down a hill. He landed in a ravine, bruised but alive.

Rain began to fall. The grey clouds were scudding away from the scene of horror. The SS executioners headed for a new life. For them the war was over. They discarded their SS uniforms, changing them

*for civilian clothes. They disappeared in the darkness of the night. The
rain kept falling intermittently.*

*April 11, 1945. The shy rays of sun penetrated the clouds. Long
shafts of light were gliding through the majestic branches of the forest
trees. The birds, inspired by the warm touch of spring, were chirping
impatiently. Several American tanks cautiously approached the forest
glade. There was an eerie stillness around. Some of the tank crew
jumped off their tanks.*

*"O God! Look what they did to those poor people, these damned
Krauts!" Captain John Simpson, in his late twenties, crossed himself
repeatedly. He was in state of a shock. He had never seen such a gruesome sight. He had fought on the beaches of Normandy, he had taken
part in many vicious battles, but here was sheer slaughter of innocent
people, mass execution, which has nothing to do with fighting a war.
Human skeletons cut down in a rage of insanity.*

*"I wish I could put my hands on these monsters, I would cut off
their balls," said one of the tank commanders.*

*Some soldiers were weeping, saying prayers for the dead. The si-
lence around was interrupted by the fluttering wings of a scared bird.
Orders were given to bring heavy equipment to open graves for mass
burial. Nameless people, no nationality, no tombs ever to be erected.*

14

KIBBUTZ EILON

A MONTH after liberation I was still languishing in Buchenwald, sleeping in the same barrack. I was surrounded by alien people speaking languages I didn't understand. All my friends from Czestochowa had perished during the death march from Buchenwald to Dachau, including my brother. Buchenwald was a big mess and the initial chaos couldn't be controlled by the American authorities because of a lack of medicine, doctors and even proper food for the starving inmates. For some inmates the newly won freedom was the beginning of the end. About three thousand died from various maladies; they collapsed like marathon runners at the end of their treks.

My freedom allowed me to come and go, but where was I supposed to go? I didn't have any money or relatives; how could I provide for myself? The camp was getting emptier by the day but I was still there waiting to leave this former domain of hell. The wounds were still fresh and my brother was on my mind. He didn't leave my thoughts for a minute. He was gone, the last link with my past.

In addition, to my great horror, I found that I was stuttering. The trauma was finally taking a toll. I was afraid that this speech problem might ruin my life, my relationships, the possibility of meeting a girl. How could I declare my love with a stutter? How could I stand before a class in school? For hours I would face a mirror, speaking slowly, trying to pronounce tricky words. A memory from school came to me of Demosthenes, the Athenian orator who used pebbles in his mouth to avoid stuttering.

Overwhelmed by recurrent spells of despair I sat numb next to my barrack, warming my bones in the spring sun, watching nature coming back to life: cherry trees in full blossom, birds crossing the sky in search of new nests.

Finally, as May came to an end, I was sent with a group of orphans to a huge camp in Metz, France where many former inmates were waiting to be repatriated to their home countries. I couldn't go back to Poland; nobody was waiting for me, nobody would want me. I wanted to go to Switzerland but the UNRRA representative was adamant: only the very sick or very young would be allowed to enter Switzerland. I even tried to enter the Swiss train but was forced back by border police. I was supposed to go to Palestine and join a Youth Aliyah in a kibbutz, any kibbutz. It wasn't my choice; orphans didn't make decisions, it was decided by someone else. I was reluctant to go, knowing only too well that I would not be able to pursue my studies there.

I loved Metz and the people there. They were warm and willing to help, although their economic situation was far from comfortable. People willing to help don't have to be rich, though. I got some pocket money from the camp administration and I strolled aimlessly through the beautiful streets of the city, indulging in the long, crisp French breads. (Since then I've never been indifferent to any bakery.) I enjoyed my lonely walks and I watched the majestic Moselle River flowing gracefully. There were trees and the blue sky wide open to my view, no barbed wire. I still couldn't comprehend my freedom and my heart would pound at the sight of a uniform. Young French couples were everywhere, embracing and kissing passionately, sitting or standing, almost motionless, resembling marble statues, yet vibrant and full of life. After a while the scenes of love grew dull for me; I envied them having each other.

In Metz I met a French Jewish family, the Rubels. I vividly recall their fashionable apartment at 21 rue Pasteur. They invited me for dinner, my first decent dinner in years. The table was covered with a sparkling white tablecloth, just like in my home. We spoke in German and I found myself yearning for the magic words, "Benjamin, stay with us. We have a nice home, you can go to school, you will be a member of the family." But the words never came and I was too shy to make the proposal myself. Rejection could be embarrassing for all of us. Perhaps they thought I would be problematic, carrying the trauma of the war with difficulties in adapting. We parted with a warm embrace.

In the camp I found some friends planning to go to Palestine and in July I boarded a ship, the *Maratoa*, for the trip there, still under British mandate. I arrived on July 24, 1945 and was received by my uncle Jehuda Bender and my distant cousin Meir Kleiman, a high ranking officer in the British Police Corps. My stay in his house was brief and my reception was cool. (There was not too much understanding at that time for Holocaust survivors. The Israeli pioneers viewed us with disdain for being led meekly to the slaughterhouses of Treblinka and Auschwitz.) He didn't need an addition to his family despite the fact that he was building a new home. He searched desperately for a kibbutz with a youth group and after a couple of weeks he was successful.

My first encounter with commune life was traumatic. Kibbutz Eilon was newly established, perhaps a couple of years old, and was surrounded by mountains resembling the Swiss Alps. But the prevailing conditions were a far cry from Switzerland. The kibbutz was poor, trying to make it on its own, the access roads unpaved, the food scarce and limited. We had bread, oranges, and soup; an egg was for two people, with a couple of sardines. This wasn't enough for hard physical work. The kibbutz was surrounded by barbed wire, a painful reminder of the past.

The morning call to work came with the sound of a bell. Eventually the initial shock gave way to a more rational view. We were a group of about forty youngsters from all over Europe: boys and girls from Poland, Russia, Romania, Hungary, Czechoslovakia, Lithuania, Belgium, France, Yugoslavia, Germany. In no time, love began to bloom, couples embracing in the evenings and disappearing in the darkness of night.

I was working, reading, studying Hebrew, trying with all my power to recapture the time lost. My job was in an orchard ploughing the soil with a mule on the rocky slopes. I also worked in a vineyard where I had to be careful not to damage the roots of the ripening grapes while ploughing, which required some skill. I was at peace with myself, enjoying the sweet solitude in the company of my mule with whom I found an excellent rapport. I treated him like a human being and he repaid me with absolute obedience. I shared my oranges and bread with him. I never hit him and I spoke to him softly like a friend. When I rested, lying on the ground, I would watch the birds, free to fly and go anywhere, crossing sealed borders to build their nests everywhere. There were moments, when I opened the sails of my memory to a new wind, that my eyes would fill with tears.

I had a teacher, Sara Weisel, who taught me Hebrew and Hebrew literature outside of school. It was her idea to help make my adaptation process much quicker, to instill in me confidence in myself. She was married to a kibbutznik, a teacher like herself, from Egypt. He spoke Hebrew, French, Arabic and English and she spoke Hebrew, Polish, and English. She tried her best to make my life bearable. She brought me books, trying to open a small window to a better world. She taught me Hebrew on her own time. This was not easy: my first contact with Hebrew was there in the kibbutz. She tried to console me when I was depressed and feeling worthless. She was more than a teacher. She tried to understand my pain, my dark past and my drive for a better future. Her only brother had perished at Buchenwald and she found similarities between us.

Each day, after half a day of work and a half a day of studies on the high school level, all the boys and girls would meet in a mini auditorium to exchange views revolving around the ideas of the Hashomer Hatzair party, the left wing in multi-party Israeli politics. At the time the party was under the spell of Russian communism. I had no interest in political meetings which I considered boring and futile. I felt that my stay in the kibbutz would be transitory, and I wasn't interested in a political life or taking orders in the name of high ideals to serve party interests. The youth group in Kibbutz Eilon was supposed to stay for two years and then join another Hashomer Hatzair kibbutz as *Haschlama*, which meant being incorporated into

Members of Kibbutz Eilon Youth Aliyah in 1947.
Benjamin is seated in the second row, second from the right,
and Sara is standing directly behind him.

a new kibbutz short of manpower. This was the concept of kibbutz life. After a year in the kibbutz, I had an excellent command of Hebrew, thanks to Sara Weisel. I was gaining confidence, beginning to draw and write, and I was ready to embark on a new life.

Sara Malachowski arrived in the kibbutz in February 1946. She had a cousin there, Grunia, who had left Poland as a pioneer before the war and was a member of Mapam. Sara had managed to make her way from Poland to Berlin and then to Paris with the help of her cousin Israel (the brother of Motzik, with whom she traveled). From there they went to Marseilles to catch a boat across the Mediterranean to Palestine. The kibbutz was only a two hour drive from the Haifa harbor. My first encounter with Sara was uneventful, but I felt an unexpected surge of awakening. She was attractive, with big brown eyes and black hair. There was something that drew me to her. To my surprise, she spoke Hebrew fluently. She soon had many admirers and I was left in the cold with my shy budding feelings.

Sara loved the kibbutz life. She was well adjusted and accepted. Our views were very different, lacking a common denominator. She was prepared to stay in the kibbutz and establish a family. I was alienated from the commune life; it was too close, with a uniform mentality forged by party requirements. Despite this, our relationship grew stronger and there was a real love flowing from our shared suffering and respect for each other.

Sara was friendly and outgoing but the kibbutz life took a heavy toll on her. Work in the huge kibbutz kitchen was hard, and clearing stones from the soil to prepare for planting was tedious and back breaking. At the end of the day she would be tired and she suffered from migraine headaches. I felt at a loss to help her.

Our closeness grew however. Often, after the day's work and several hours of school, we would spend hours walking together arm in arm in the orchard. My love for Sara brought a dramatic change in my behavior. Occasionally I would bring her the best fruits from the orchard and the vineyard; on my rare days off I would buy her some Palmolive soap or Nivea cream in Haifa or Hedera. She bought me swimming trunks. The bouts of depression began to disappear, as did the stuttering. I was in love and felt that I was loved.

Kibbutz Eilon was growing. The kibbutz had, in addition to the orchard and vineyard, a factory that produced water meters and agricultural equipment. The food got a little better, but not much. As a group of mostly orphaned Holocaust survivors, we were performing well, perhaps too well. There was an interest in good performance but not much attention to the conditions. My work in the vineyard was hard and unhealthy: I used to spray the grapes with sulphur, sometimes in the wind, and I would walk in clouds of sulphur without a mask for hours.

I was always happy to get back to the kibbutz to take a shower in the kind of tin boxes we had. The boys' shower was full of holes covered with pieces of soap. Some of the boys would peep through the holes to the girls' shower. This strenuous one-eye effort caused them heart palpitations and a surge of expectations that never came true.

To everyone's delight, an Olympic-sized swimming pool was built when the kibbutz could afford it. Sara and I learned to swim and enjoyed the water's coolness in the hot, humid evenings. We used to go to the pool late, when no one was there except us. Swimming wasn't the only objective; we would stand together embracing in the water, kissing passionately, our hair dripping water and our hearts pounding. Above our heads the silver moon would glide through the indigo sky studded with glimmering stars. These precious moments of happiness took us away from the daily difficulties to thoughts of a better life lurking somewhere on the distant horizon.

After about a year in the kibbutz the whole group took a trip with our teachers to explore and see the beauty of the land of our ancestors. We walked for two weeks in the mountains, sleeping on the ground at night, covered with blankets. We were accompanied by a few members of the elite Palmach units

(*Plugot Mahatz*—crack troops) who carried arms. There were moments of danger and unexpected pitfalls. One of our teachers disappeared at one point. He had fallen into a deep cave and we had to lift him up with a heavy line. He was okay but shook up a bit. Some couldn't take the harsh ordeal of the trip. The strong always helped the weak.

One day at sunset we arrived at Jericho. We were walking into ancient history, remembering the words of the bible when the walls tumbled and the trumpets sounded. The sun, a huge fireball, was coming down slowly on the horizon, setting the sky ablaze. Arabs were sitting around a fire puffing on their pipes, motionless, watching the flames. Their camels stood next to them resembling statues. The scene was mystifying, full of whispers. Occasionally the barking of a dog from far away would pierce the stillness. Nothing had changed here for ages, everything had remained the same: the sand, the rocks, the sky, the lonely tree, leafless, scorched by the desert sun. At that moment I felt very close to the land of Israel. We went as far as Kali on the Dead Sea.

Life in the kibbutz was tough, but there were moments of elation. In the dining room was an old piano used only on special festival occasions, but Johanan, from Austria, played piano and accordian and formed a singing group of mostly girls, with a few boys, myself included. He was very fond of German *Gemutliche* music. Sara had a good voice, as did most of the girls. When we sang these nostalgic tunes there was a total change of atmosphere. We came together and were able to reminisce about the good days of the past. Often we would also go to the kitchen and the bakery and get oranges and bread, enough to satisfy the constant hunger. On free week-

*Youth members of Kibbutz Eilon during a two week trip to the
Judea Mountains and Jericho, Palestine, April, 1947.*

end days we would gather together and dance to Johanan's
accordian accompaniment. Just the hora, no other dances like
the tango or the English waltz were allowed in the kibbutz
where it was a kind of spartan life—no smoking, no playing
cards, no discussions about sex. On many occasions the rhythm
got stronger and stronger, and breathless, sweating profusely,
we were ashamed to leave the ring. Sara was a good dancer
too; she even took part in the annual dance festival at Kibbutz
Dalia.

In my free time I would sit in the culture house, a kind of
library, studying books, learning English by myself, trying my
hand at drawing with some success. I wrote some short stories
in Polish, which were translated by my teacher.

Almost every evening there were group discussions revolving around the life in a kibbutz. We were supposed to be pioneers adhering to the lofty ideals of a kibbutz life. Some of us
found these discussions boring, but no one wanted to be the

black sheep so everyone tried to show up. The lofty, somehow hollow ideas didn't appeal to me. I wasn't ready to accept them at that stage of my life. I was infatuated with independent thinking, to be free like a bird. I was haunted by bad memories of minds twisted to the requirements of the state and its leaders. I wanted to reach my own conclusions, using my own judgment for better or for worse.

At a very important kibbutz ceremony I was the only one not to take the oath of allegiance to the party. The next day I was ridiculed and verbally attacked. No one could understand my defiance; I was an excellent worker, a good student. My goal was to establish an independent life, to be a good provider and to make Sara happy. The loss of the sweetness of home, surrounded by love, lingered in my mind.

There were ominous signs that a bloody confrontation between Arabs and Jews was in the making. Arabs, sensing the imminent departure of the British from Palestine, were attacking Jewish settlers. Cases of rape and murder were common. The Palmach units would often capture the perpetrators; the murderers were eliminated and the rapists were castrated. The law of the Bible and the Koran was an eye for an eye. The children of Abraham still couldn't find a common understanding.

In the middle of 1947 I decided to leave the kibbutz. This step was painful and perhaps brutal for us. I was leaving Sara in pursuit of some foggy personal ambition. There was the possibility that I would lose her to someone else; there was a waiting line of young batchelors ready to exploit a suitable opportunity. I was torn, not knowing which way to go. My ambitions were still unclear.

After I left I had to come to grips with another struggle,

survival. I worked for a time in the storage room of a British police station on the recommendation of my cousin Meir. I attended the Aliantz school to obtain my degree. But I could hardly make ends meet. I left that job to work in the harbour as a longshoreman, carrying burlap bags heavy with fish flour. The stench was unbearable and the Arabs from Kurdistan working with us smelled of onion and garlic. They worked almost naked with two pieces of burlap attached with wire covering their front and back. They were in top condition and would walk a steep, narrow board leading to the trucks. I could hardly do it, my legs trembling. Here I was alone, feeling that my back would break at any moment. I was ashamed to leave. I needed the money badly.

In November of 1947 the UN declared the partition of Palestine, half of the land to the Arabs, and half to the Jews. The Arabs rejected the solution and this meant the prelude to a bloody war with unpredictable results. On May 14, 1948, the Arab combined forces of Egypt, Syria, Iraq, Lebanon, Yemen, and Saudi Arabia attacked the new state of Israel. They carried the banners of a new Holocaust: "We will throw you into the sea."

I joined Palmach, the nucleus of the future Israeli Defense Force (IDF). Sara, having left the kibbutz to be with her mother in Sabinia, near Haifa, joined a signal unit in the north. We were separated. Three years after the Holocaust we were back at war for our lives and the independence of the Israeli state.

15

A WEDDING PROMISE

THE SOUTHERN NEGEV desert in the fall of 1948 was a scene of heavy fighting. No one could imagine the outcome of this struggle. The war was fought by many against few. The combined Arab forces tried to eliminate the new-born State of Israel once and for all. But the Egyptians were being hit relentlessly by the Palmach units. The Egyptians who mercilessly pounded kibbutz Yad Mordechai were running for their lives, leaving their positions in haste. The battlefield was littered with shoes. It was inconceivable to walk on the hot sands barefoot, but the Egyptians did it.

In October, the desert began to turn cold. The days were still hot, but the nights were freezing. I had reason to be happy though. I had received a letter from Sara with a certificate confirmed by the Rabbi of Kiryat Motzkin. The prelude to our marriage had been short. Our wedding was to take place on October 14, 1948. The war was still raging, soldiers were getting killed, but in spite of that we decided to marry. I studied the Rabbi's certificate. I would have to report to my commanding officer, or a higher up, to get permission to marry. During the war, normal affairs turn out to be less normal. Military regulations were cumbersome and insurmountable.

"Benjamin, a letter from a loved one," somebody interrupted my thoughts. I turned around, caught red-handed. Moshe, my close friend, was standing next to me, smiling. Moshe, like me, was a Holocaust survivor.

"Moshe, I received the pre-wedding certificate," I said anxiously.

"Smile, be happy," Moshe exulted.

"Moshe, I have mixed feelings about the forthcoming affair, they won't let me go. Tomorrow we are supposed to storm Beersheba."

Moshe began to giggle.

"Moshe, why are you giggling for God's sake, it makes me mad," I said angrily.

"Benjamin, do you know what we used to say in Katowice?"

"Probably something very smart," I said, folding the certificate.

"Well not exactly words of wisdom, but something very practical. 'A person shouldn't worry before, only after.'"

"You're right," I said, "It makes sense."

"Okay, I have to go," Moshe said, departing.

On October 13, I requested an appointment with the battalion Commander. The appointment was granted. I donned my new uniform, shaved, and combed my unruly hair, quite a job. My boots were shiny. I even changed my torn shoelaces, trying to assume a good appearance. Fifteen minutes ahead of time I reported to the commander's secretary. She picked up the telephone.

"Rafi, Benjamin Bender is here to see you…okay, go in," the secretary said.

My heart was pounding. I knocked on the door.

"Come in."

I opened the door, took a few steps forward, saluted, gave my name and rank, and then folded my hands behind my back. The battalion commander was in his late twenties, dressed in a casual way, his appearance somewhat disheveled. He didn't lift his eyes, studying some papers. "What's the problem?" he uttered dryly.

"I have my wedding on October 14. After one day I will be back in my unit, only one day," I concluded quickly.

The battalion commander lifted his eyes from the papers and gave me a long look. "Well, you have a strong case," he began, "but we are going to storm Beersheba. We are in a war, personal matters which might be of importance to you are secondary, and are of no importance when matters of state are involved. You will have to wait patiently and postpone the wedding."

"But commander, I gave a promise. We will have only a *minyan* (in Jewish tradition, the required quorum of ten men)." I was desperately trying to make a point. "We are both Holocaust survivors, I have no parents. My future wife has only a mother, please, one day," I pleaded.

The battalion commander was adamant. "I am sorry, although you have a valid case, I cannot make any exceptions. There are quite a few similar cases on my desk. The answer is no."

There was nothing I could say. I saluted and left the room. I felt humiliated, broken, disappointed. How could I humiliate a bride—it was even against Jewish law? The fate of the state was weighing on my shoulders. "Personal matters are secondary," just like that. Everything was secondary, Buchenwald, loss of my parents, loss of my brother, and now loss of the wedding.

Suddenly the spell of weakness evaporated. I regained my strength. I was twenty. Since the age of thirteen, somebody else played Russian roulette with my life. Everyone, state officials, commanders, everyone except me. I was born to be a pawn, to obey, to shut up, to listen and behave, with the constant threat of punishment. If jail was the answer, so be it. This would not be my loss, but the state's loss. Soldiers are needed on the front line, not in jails. I made up my mind to escape, the commander didn't leave me any choice.

"Benjamin!" somebody was hollering. I turned around. Moshe was approaching. "Benjamin, what happened?" Moshe asked.

"This is what happened, it wasn't supposed to happen," I answered, agitated. "The commander won't allow me to go, but I will surprise him, because I intend to go."

"Benjamin, don't get upset, I will help you." Moshe was trying to calm me down.

"Thank you."

"I will take care of your personal equipment. If we can't falsify a pass, you will have to hide under the cover of darkness and then you will leave the camp through the Burma road (the escape route). You will have to be extremely cautious because if they catch you, you'll go to jail before the wedding. They won't allow you a jail wedding. It's preferable to go to jail after the wedding, then at least you can indulge in sweet memories." Moshe concluded jokingly.

"Moshe, stop this nonsense, you are lucky not to be in my shoes," I stopped him.

"Benjamin, no, no, please, you are perfectly right, to hell with them. You are entitled to a small portion of happiness.

We will win the battle without you. Let's go to work," Moshe added.

I began to fold my scout tent. My anxiety was growing rapidly, with foreboding that my escape mission might fail. "Moshe, here is my kitbag, the blanket is inside, always the blanket, no end to it. I'll just take my backpack."

We embraced. "Good luck," Moshe said. "Do you know the approach to the Burma road?"

"Yes, I know." Every army camp had its Burma road. We waved. I left the camp, heading for the fields. The units of the military police were already patrolling the area. I knew the escape route well. It would take me no more than thirty minutes to reach the road. I was furious. I had suffered all my life, never a bright moment, never a moment of joy, an uphill fight to preserve my damned life, to serve the interests of others. I was walking through freshly opened furrows. The earth was soft, tender. I was sweating profusely, moist soil sticking to my boots. I headed north.

The moment I reached the road, I would have to hitchhike, the only free transportation for a penniless soldier. Darkness descended quickly. From far away, I saw the passing lights of trucks moving in different directions. For some reason, the faces of my deceased parents came to my mind. They didn't have to go through many ordeals. They had committed suicide. The asphalt road gleamed in the moonlight. I began to run, seeing a moving light. It seemed to be a truck, the light beams were far apart from each other. I stood on the road's soft shoulder. I took off my hat and began to wave desperately. The truck was getting very close, slowing down and coming to a full stop. This wasn't a military vehicle, but a private con-

struction truck, bearing the inscription Shelev. The truck driver was in his fifties.

"Where do you want to go?"

"To Sabinia, after Mifratz Haifa, but please try to avoid
check points, I am AWOL. I left my unit without permission
to get married." I said, taking a deep breath, not wanting to
lie to the driver.

"Wait," said the driver, "I'll move my truck a little bit closer
to the shoulder of the road. I can't promise you VIP treatment,
as a groom deserves, but I will bring you safely to Mifratz
Haifa," the driver said, giving me a soft fatherly look. "On the
truck you will find a heap of burlap bags, cover yourself thor-
oughly underneath. The military police are swarming all over
the roads. There are probably many more weddings and dare-
devils like you."

"Thank you." I said, jumping expertly on the truck.

The air was chilly and moist. I went underneath the dusty
jute bags. I didn't care. The bags were being used to transport
sand, or small pebbles to constructions sites. The truck was
moving swiftly, giving me a good shake. I was sweating profusely. The huge heap of burlap bags was like a fence. I covered myself with several bags, a kind of blanket, some I folded
under my head, creating the illusion of a pillow. Before I went
to sleep, I urinated in the direction of the wind. Poor driver,
his window was open. I curled up like a dog. I was thinking
about Sara, who had written me a couple days earlier. "The
wedding will be only with a *minyan*, and we will wear our
military uniforms. I will wear a wedding veil only." Her letter
was sad, but this was the reality, no parents to help, to care. I
didn't care, the wedding ceremony was short lived, the real

*Sara Malachowski and Benjamin Bender
on their wedding day, Israel, 1948.*

thing is the celebration of life. We would love each other, that's
what counted. I slumped into a deep sleep.

The truck came to a sudden halt. The jute bags fell over my
head. I got up and stretched my numbed limbs. I felt sand in
my mouth.

"We are at our destination," the driver announced happily.

"It went amazingly quickly," I said with gratitude in my
voice.

"Not so quickly as you might think, the military police
stopped me three times, checking the truck with flash lights,
but everything went smoothly," the driver said proudly.

"I don't know how to thank you. I hope one of these days
we will meet under different circumstances."

"I hope so, meanwhile *mazel tov*, have a big family, we need
lots of babies," the driver said.

The driver bid me farewell and disappeared in the pitch dark. I was at Mifratz Haifa, with another twenty-five minutes to Sabinia. I was standing next to the bus stop. I checked my pockets desperately. There were some coins, just enough for one fare. I didn't have to wait too long, the bus arrived within minutes. I stepped into the bus, handing the driver the exact fare.

"Sabinia."

"You're lucky," said the driver, handing me a ticket, "this is the last bus."

The bus was almost empty. Two passengers were sitting in the back. A chilly wind blew through the open window. I closed my eyes. Sara was unaware that I was coming. I couldn't call, Israel in 1948 was without private telephones. I couldn't write, there wasn't time and the mail delivery was slow. It was about a hundred yards from the bus stop to Sara's house. I ran.

Sara was standing outside the small modest *Schikun* (condo unit) she was living in with her mother. She began to run towards me. We embraced, kissing each other with tenderness. My eyes were moist. She looked into them.

"Benjamin, I was worried about you," she uttered her words in a whisper.

"I know, I almost failed in my wedding mission," I said kissing her face. "Sara, I am AWOL, they didn't let me go, even for one day. I escaped with Moshe's help. I might face a court marshal, but I don't really care, I gave my share in many battles. If they put me in jail, I will have a good time far away from the front line," I concluded.

"Why are they so cruel, you just asked for one day?" Sara said with anguish.

"In wars there are no whys. My battalion commander said that personal matters are secondary. When I left his room, I knew exactly what I would do. In this case my personal, or rather our personal matters are first." The full moon was gliding like a sailboat amidst the clouds. We stood looking at each other. "Sara, are we doing the right thing, I mean the timing? After the wedding ceremony I am going back to the front line," I said sadly.

Sara was immersed in thoughts. "Yes, Benjamin, we are doing the right thing, we love each other. We have a mission to accomplish in our lives, this is only the beginning," she said, her voice rising.

The next day we were wed. There was barely a *minyan*, but in the last moment a tenth person appeared. Rabbi Vogelmann of Kiryat Motzkin gave us his blessings. Sara and I wore our military uniforms. Sara's head was covered with a thin veil. I broke the glass firmly and signed a *Ktuva*, a marriage certificate with an obligatory note for fifty Israeli pounds. I looked curiously at the writing on the *Ktuva*: "You will see the light of life with a wife you love." The sentence had deep meaning.

The short wedding ceremony had a hint of sadness, no relatives, or friends, only people to form a *minyan*. Even my uncle from Hedera wasn't present. There had been no assurance that the wedding would take place. One day after the wedding I returned to my unit, accompanied by Sara. Lacking transportation, we wound up on the top of a tow truck. We couldn't sit so we stood all the way.

The Ber Yacov camp was deserted. Sara's presence didn't soften the harsh verdict. I was court marshalled and dispatched promptly to the front line. During the Israeli War of Independence, the jails were empty. The front line didn't have room for reflections. Sara returned home and then joined her army unit. After the wedding there was no honeymoon. I had to pay my dues for my country. Duty first, love and marriage second, but the wedding promise wasn't broken.

16

HONEYMOON

THE EMBATTLED Negev that winter was reminiscent of shifting desert dunes. The battle grounds were changing rapidly. The swift and efficient Palmach units were exerting pressure on the very footsteps of the retreating Egyptian forces. New names cropped up, strange names never heard before. Names like Mash Rafah, Migdal, Udz el Hafir, Um Katef, Abu Ageila, Rafiah, Dir Aslud'z, Maaleh Akrabim, Ein Husub. Six months had passed since Sara and I had been married in a very simple ceremony. I kept my promise to write to Sara before every battle and after. She was always on my mind.

I was beset by nagging doubts. Where was Sara now? She was serving in the signal corp at the northern front. Was she faithful to me? She was pretty, attractive, friendly, and there was a war. War brings loneliness. Soldiers far from home are searching for a warm touch, for consolation. Death is a close companion undermining the true value of love.

We were married the very day Beersheba was taken from the Egyptians. During the war romances were blooming and wilting. Soldiers were getting married at an unprecedented rate. There was a feeling that war would make the bonds of love stronger…

———

SARA WAS despondent. She couldn't understand why all the letters she wrote were unanswered. Benjamin never failed to write, this wasn't his nature. She began to worry, unaware that their mail was winding up in the mine fields. She tried to share her doubts with her mother. Her mother consoled her but there was hardly a sign of moral support.

One day Sara made up her mind. She had to find him at any price. February in the Negev is not a pleasant month. Roads turned to clay mud, trucks could hardly move. No adequate roads were being paved in 1949. Only a jeep, or a scout car could move in this ocean of mud. The torrential rains spelled misery. On Monday the tenth, she reported to her commanding officer, without asking for a formal appointment. Her commanding officer Yudith Kleinman was her best friend. They knew each other well. Yudith was short, a *Sabra* (Israeli born), and she had straight brown hair, a small nose, brown eyes, and a pleasant round face.

"Yudith, I need two weeks furlough," Sara said hesitantly.

"Two weeks?" Yudith repeated, stunned. "What for?" she added.

"I must find Benjamin."

"Don't worry about him, he's okay."

"Yudith, I am worried, something is wrong. I have to see him with my own eyes."

"Do you at least know where he is?" Yudith stared at Sara with compassion.

"I am not sure, he was stationed in Beersheba with the Ninth Battalion of the Palmach."

"Sara it's not so simple. How will you be able to reach Beersheba? With all my good intentions I cannot offer you a tank. The roads are muddy, unpassable. You will get stuck in nowhere, and then what?"

"Yudith," Sara pleaded, "Do I have a choice? Put yourself in my situation, Benjamin is my husband, I have to know if he is still alive," Sara concluded firmly.

"Okay Sara, you've made your point, I have no objections anymore, but you'll still have to solve some logistical problems of transportation…this is entirely up to you," Yudith said, handing her a furlough permit.

"Thank you, Yudith, I will always remember this favor." Sara said, wiping away tears.

"Stop it," Yudith said, visibly moved. "Go and find him, this is an order." They embraced warmly.

Upon arriving home, Sara again tried to share her anxiety with her mother.

"Mama, I have decided to go look for Benjamin," she said firmly.

"Are you out of your mind, in the middle of the war you are going to look for him? No, you are not going!"

"Mama, I have to go, he is my husband, I worry about him."

"You are out of your mind, a woman, alone, going to the front line, you can get killed before finding him. Do you realize what you are getting yourself into?"

"Yes I know exactly what I am doing, this is final," Sara said firmly.

"You want to go, go, but remember I warned you not to."

Sara didn't answer, she was used to this kind of talk. If her father had been alive, he would understand her decision. Sara went to bed very early. She set her alarm clock. There was no question in her mind that she was undertaking a dangerous task. She got up early, even before the alarm clock buzzed. She took a shower and straightened out her bed. She opened her closet and donned her dark green military uniform, an American surplus contribution to the State of Israel. She took her oxford shoes, putting on white socks. She checked and rechecked her little handbag. Her mother was still asleep, she didn't want to wake her.

Sara left Kiryat Motzkin early. She didn't have to wait too long. A scout car took her to Haifa. From Haifa she was supposed to get to Rechovot, heading south to Beersheba, a six hour drive. The rain stopped, but the road was wet and slippery. Occasionally heavy equipment went by on huge ramps. It took her one hour to get to Haifa. The scout car driver was gliding on the road, driving at a very high speed. From Haifa a tow truck took her to Hatzor. So far everything was proceeding smoothly. She looked at herself, her dark green American uniform immaculate, brass buttons shining in the grey light of the day. At Hatzor the tow truck driver dropped her off, looking at her with some amazement. The roads were deserted, except for military vehicles moving speedily. Sara stood at Hatzor's bus stop. The warm rays of sun penetrated the gloomy sky. There was a fragrance of flowers and the smell of open furrows. The black asphalt was gleaming and steaming. Her anxiety was gone, she felt confident that she had done the right thing. With all the initial difficulties life was good, holding a promise of happiness. A military truck was closing in rapidly. Sara began to wave her hand to slow him down. The truck stopped with a squeak.

"Where do you want to go?" the driver asked, bending over the open window.

"To Beersheba."

"I can take you only to the intersection of Kibbutz Saad."

"Okay, good enough," Sara said, ascending the cabin of the truck.

The driver stared at her curiously. She was probably too elegant in her American uniform. The driver was a Yemenite. He had curly black hair, black glowing eyes. Around his neck, he wore a gold chain with a Star of David. A good omen.

"My name is Menachem," the driver said.

"I'm Sara."

"What are you doing in this damned place?" Menachem asked curiously, without moving his eyes from her.

"I'm looking for my husband. We just got married recently...I lost touch with him."

"Do you have any possible clues, where he is supposed to be?"

"As far as I know he was stationed at Beersheba. His battalion took Beersheba."

"Ah, now I know, he is a Palmachnik. Don't worry, you will find him." Menachem said reassuringly.

Rain began to fall again. The blue sky retained the misty veil of gloom. There was a depressing silence.

"Do you have a family?" Sara asked.

"Yes, I have a large family, five brothers and four sisters. We are a very close family. I have a girl friend, we hope to marry after the war. As a matter of fact my girl friend insisted that we should marry right away. I refused. I am sorry, I shouldn't have said this," he concluded.

Sara didn't say a word, immersed in thoughts. She stared aimlessly at the fleeting road. They passed neat villages, green fields, stretching as far as the eyes can see. Israeli ingenuity was outstanding, they had succeeded in changing an arid desert into a blooming garden. But would the ancient prophecy ever turn out to be true: would the people of Israel change their swords to ploughshares?

"We are not far from Kibbutz Saad. For your next lift you will have to wait in the open field. I hope it doesn't rain," Menachem said braking his truck. The truck stopped abruptly. "This is as far as I can take you. Saad is right over there," he pointed at the cluster of spawning small homes, surrounded by greenery.

"Thank you, Menachem."

"Sara, good luck, take care."

She was alone, in the middle of nowhere. She stood on the soft shoulder of the road, her beautiful oxford shoes sinking in the rusty sticky soil. The road was deserted, except little figures of people working laboriously in the distant fields.

Darkness in the south descends unexpectedly. She prayed silently that she would reach Beersheba before nightfall. If worse came to worst, she would walk to the kibbutz and ask for shelter. During the War of Independence, the various kibbutzim were the backbone of the young state. They gave the best they had: soldiers, officers, generals, ministers, scholars and writers.

Again Sara looked at the road. From far away, a small point was growing bigger and bigger. Her heart pounded with hope and expectation. The shape got clearer. This was undoubtedly a jeep. The question was how many soldiers were in the jeep—

if there were four, everything was lost. The jeep was closing in rapidly.

She couldn't believe her eyes, her heart filling with joy. She counted three persons in the jeep. The jeep stopped next to her. She stepped back, trying to avoid the splash of the mud. The three military men in the jeep were high ranking officers, very young, maybe in their twenties.

"Where are you going in this kind of a weather?" one of them asked.

"I am heading for Beersheba, can you give me a lift?"

"Of course, there is one unoccupied seat…we just dropped off another hitchhiker."

Sara jumped in.

"Let me introduce everyone," said the driver. "My name is Avigdor, this is Schlomo and Avram." They looked curiously at her American uniform, which had been just introduced for the *Chen* (*Cheil Hanashim*—the women's army). "Do you have any particular reason to visit Beersheba at this time of year? Forgive me for my intruding question, you look like an American soldier; I'm seeing this kind of uniform for the first time," Avigdor concluded.

"Well, I just got this uniform recently. I am serving in the signal unit, at the northern front. I am looking for my husband. We married recently. One day after the wedding he joined his unit." Sara didn't want to tell the whole story. "I hope he is well, I haven't heard from him for a long time."

Avigdor looked at Sara at length.

"Is his name Benjamin?" he asked, smiling.

"Yes, yes!" Sara blurted out, her heart pounding. She looked at Avigdor, somewhat disoriented. "Now I see!" she exclaimed,

Sara, on the ground, third from the right,
training with a youth group in Israel, 1948.

looking at the left side of his shirt. Avigdor was bearing a small red triangle, the emblem of Benjamin's unit, the Ninth Battalion, the motorized unit of Palamach. "Avigdor, tell me the truth, is Benjamin alive?"

"Of course he is alive, but I am not sure you will find him in Beersheba."

Sara was devastated. After this inhuman ordeal, the road was widening again.

"I think he is in Ein Husub, in the vicinity of Sodom. He participated in Operation Uvda-Eilath. There is only one road to get there and a very bad one at that. You will have to sleep over in Beersheba. The next day, try to get in touch with him by telegram. I don't think that you will be able to reach him in Ein Husub. The unpaved road at Maaleh Akrabim is quite dangerous, the curves are treacherous. Quite a few Studebakers have found their graves in the ravine. Only the most skillful

drivers can challenge those curves. After reaching Beersheba,"
Avigdor added, "I am going back to Tel Aviv, my room is va-
cant. I will give orders to prepare the room for you."

"Thank you, Avigdor," Sara said.

They entered Beersheba. Only recently the place had been
a scene of heavy fighting. Beersheba was demolished. Many
Arab homes were burned down, charred trees seemed like they
had been hit by a thunder storm. The houses were in colors,
some were pink, yellow. Donkeys were strolling apathetically,
braying occasionally. Broken glass was all over, refuse of discarded belongings, smashed doors, open trenches in the street,
silent testimony to the raging street fights. Sara thought fleet-
ingly about the families, living here for generations. They had
left their homes with no hope of return.

The jeep stopped at the market place, adjacent to a pink villa,
now occupied by Benjamin's unit. Outside the villa was a sign,
"Dr. Ahmed Mansur." Sara entered the Mansur house. The villa
was spacious with many rooms. The house was built out of
Jerusalem stones; the Arabs were excellent stonemasons. The
rooms were filled with Israeli soldiers. They stared at her, whistling with amusement.

"Where is the commanding officer?" she asked one of the
soldiers.

"Itzhak Quadrat is in the next room, right here." The soldier pointed to the left.

She knocked on the door.

"Come in." Itzhak Quadrat was alone in his room. He was
sitting behind a teak table, probably Dr. Mansur's working
table. Quadrat looked at her with growing astonishment.
Quadrat was wearing glasses, his chin square; with his small

narrow eyes, he had the appearance of a teacher. He didn't look like a Palmach officer. "Well, well, what can I do for you?"

"I am looking for my husband, Benjamin Bender. I haven't heard from him for the past six months."

"Benjamin is alive and well," Quadrat said, trying to dispel her anxiety. "I am sorry, to reach him will be impossible, he is in Ein Husub, close to Sodom. Please sit down," Quadrat said politely. Sara was exhausted, but she didn't accept the offered chair. "I will try to send a telegram, the lines of communications are quite bad, but I will try."

"Thank you, Itzhak," she said, leaving the room.

When she left Quadrat's room, she didn't know what to do next. As she stood immersed in thoughts, a young man approached her. He was in his twenties, tall, brown hair, a *kafiah* around his head.

"Are you Sara?" he asked.

"Yes, I am, and who are you?"

"I am Sigmund, Benjamin's friend. I know exactly where he is."

"Oh good!" Sara exclaimed.

"Listen carefully," Sigmund began. "The whole thing is not so simple, but it can be done, of course, with smart planning."

"What do you have in mind?" she asked curiously.

"Tomorrow morning, very early, about five o'clock, I am leaving for Ein Husub, with a second driver. There is no room in the cabin. The truck is a huge Studebaker, with cases of TNT. No smoking on the truck," Sigmund admonished her.

"Don't worry, I don't smoke."

"Good. Otherwise we will be on the road to heaven," he concluded jokingly.

"Sigmund, where shall I wait?"

"Outside the market place. I will move my truck a little further, nobody should see us, because I would be in deep trouble. Take a *kafiah*, it's perfect against sand storms. This will be quite a long trip, the road is very bad. In the truck you will find two blankets and a clay jug of water. It will be a little uncomfortable, but I cannot do more than that," Sigmund concluded apologetically.

"This is more than enough, I don't expect VIP treatment," Sara said, somewhat embarrassed.

They shook hands. Sigmund looked at her with respect. As he left he turned back a couple times. Sara then called Quadrat. He was evasive. He was lying, or just unable to establish contact with Benjamin. Sara was prepared to take this daring step, this was the only way she would be able to see him.

Avigdor's room was sparkling clean. The room was modest, with just a table, a chair and a small closet. The bed was immaculate. She took a shower. The physical and mental strain of the past days were taxing her strength. She went to bed, stretching out her aching limbs, thinking constantly about Benjamin. She sensed his anguish deeply, but she would see him soon, embrace him, look into his eyes. She sank into a deep slumber.

She got up after four a.m. Outside it was still dark. Through the open window a light breeze filled the room, mixed with a smell of manure from the fields. She dressed quickly, fixing the bed. She put the checkered *kafiah* of the Arab Legion over her head.

The streets were deserted. Some soldiers were attending their trucks. Sara headed towards the market place as instructed by Sigmund. The colossal Studebaker loomed in the darkness, its lights dimmed. When Sigmund saw her approaching, the truck began to move slowly in order to leave the range of the market, then it came to a full stop. The second driver jumped out of Sigmund's cabin, carrying a kind of hook-on ladder. In a matter of seconds she was on the truck.

The truck was full of explosives loaded to full capacity. She didn't care about the danger, and she didn't intend to dwell on her safety. She spread out two blankets on the floor. Sigmund had left ample room for her. People like him gave to the new-born nation the best of themselves. There was a chilly moisture in the air. She curled up in the corner of the truck, oblivious to reality, eagerly waiting for sunrise. She fell asleep.

The first rays of sun hit the truck. Sara woke up, her body numb, and she stood up, trying to catch a view. The truck was moving fast, shaking terribly. The road was bumpy. The crates of TNT were squeaking and swaying in various directions. She lifted her head towards the sky. The blazing desert sun was rising majestically in a splendor of colors. Ancient mountains, shrouded in legends, gleamed and sparkled like precious stones. A rainbow of colors: green, gold, orange, blue, red. Naked slopes, barren, deserted, but retaining the glory of ages. The tribes of Israel lived here. The fiery prophets preached here. Everything began here. She was overwhelmed by the immense beauty lurking in every corner. For thousands of years these glorious mountains were a silent witness to the survival struggle of Israel. The beginning was here on this barren land.

The sun was getting stronger. This was February, not the scorching months of July or August. She couldn't take her eyes away from the surroundings. She marveled at the old trees with the exposed roots yearning for water. The roots, rejected by the scorched earth, still clung to life, like a baby trying to suck an empty breast.

Sara's eyes rested on a small open wooden box in the corner of the truck. She lifted out a *jarra*, a clay water jug. Sigmund had figured out all the details. She lifted it above her head, opened her mouth and poured a thin stream of cold refreshing water into her mouth. She recalled the days working in the fields of Kibbutz Eilon.

The cumbersome truck came to a complete stop. They were at the highest level. She bent over the truck. The height made her dizzy.

"Hold on," Sigmund shouted, "We are backing up."

The curve was very narrow, down a deep ravine over a thousand feet deep. Sigmund, as skillful as he was, had to back at least three times before he was able to proceed. Sara looked at her gold Doxa watch, a gift from Benjamin. He had saved every *grush* (penny) from his military pay to buy her this expensive gift.

Ein Husub was quite close. Already eight hours had passed since she left Beersheba. Sara was tired, her limbs aching, eyes burning from dust and sweat. She took off her *kafiah*. She was confident that she would find Benjamin in this desolate place. The time would come when she would tell the story to her children and grandchildren. She was paying a price. Roses have thorns but they are beautiful. The land had thorns but this was the land of Israel. She wiped the sweat from her eyes. Far away down the valley, she saw a cluster of green tents, army tents, surrounded by steep slopes shooting into the sky. No more ordeals, no more surprises—in one of those tents was her husband.

The Studebaker was moving slowly down with its brakes, braving the descent with difficulty. Finally they reached the entrance of the camp. Sara jumped off the truck and looked around anxiously for a soldier. The first huge tent had an inscription *Maate*, command post. She entered the sweltering tent. Three soldiers were sitting on the bed, playing cards and drinking soda. They were visibly surprised to see her coming from nowhere.

"What is a woman soldier doing in this place?" shouted one of the soldiers.

"I am looking for my husband Benjamin Bender."

"He's not here."

"Where is he?" she asked brusquely, trying to control her growing anxiety.

"Don't worry he is nearby. I will go to relieve him. He is on guard duty." The soldier was young, maybe eighteen, blond with bushy, unkempt hair.

She left the tent, not being able to withstand the heat. The place was like a fortress, surrounded by majestic mountains, strange in shape, ravishing in a flood of colors.

The minutes passed; they seemed like hours. Finally, from a short distance, up the hill, she saw Benjamin. He was leaping, descending from the hill, trying to avoid rocks on his way. Was he aware that she was waiting for him? Maybe the soldier kept him uninformed. Suddenly he lifted his head. Their eyes met.

———

I BEGAN to run, stretching out my hands, like a bird. "Sara, Sara, I don't believe it!" We fell into each other's arms. "Sara let me look into your eyes," I said, overwhelmed by happiness. Her eyes were moist, full of tears. "Sara, why did you do it, the roads are unsafe, are you hungry or thirsty?"

"No, no, not yet. Why didn't you write?" she asked.

"Why didn't *you* write?" I repeated. We burst into loud laughter. "Thank God, all our letters were lost, otherwise I wouldn't see you here," I said, and then corrected myself. "I am not trying to be selfish," I added apologetically. We were walking, holding hands, oblivious to war. There was an eerie stillness around. We stopped every yard, embracing passionately. Everything was meaningless except this very moment. The sun, fire ball, was sinking slowly behind the mountain wall, exploding in cascade of colors. We sat down on a rock, looking with awe at God's creation.

"How is your mother?" I asked, trying to regroup my thoughts.

"Okay, she is fine."

The darkness descended rapidly. The sky, a deep, dark blue, was filled with stars. When we reached the camp, a pleasant surprise was waiting. My friends had erected a tent for us. The night was bright, and the moon began to glide frivolously behind the mountains, playing hide and seek. The small tent, built for one, this time was enough for two. Our eyes were glimmering with happiness. The long awaited honeymoon came at last.

17

THE ALTALENA INCIDENT

THE HONEYMOON wasn't quite the happy ending. The war continued with all its ferocity. I was in the Negev Desert, Israel, August 1949, during a lull in the fighting during a United Nation Security Council enforced armistice. My Palmach company was due to leave Kibbutz Gvaram for a long awaited furlough. We sat on the ground neatly dressed in beige khaki. The uniforms we wore were from U.S. Army surplus. The hats, resembling the hats of Rommel's African Corps, came from the generosity of American Jews, with love from a Jewish *hitel macher*. We carried new rifles which only recently arrived from Czechoslovakia. The bandoliers were British, as were the Sten guns and Brens. The silence of the night was interrupted by distant artillery thuds. Occasionally, hissing flares illuminated the darkness. The earth was trembling and so was our human flesh.

I was resting on the ground, spreadeagled, my hands folded behind my head. I was staring at the glimmering starry sky. At that very moment my thoughts turned to Thomas Mann's *Der Zauberberg*. The tuberculosis patients at Davos were watching the falling stars making a wish for a gift of life. A lonely star departed from the galaxy of other stars and fell into the darkness of the night. Everything was fleeting, even the life of the stars. For six months, from battle to battle, I had been waiting for a furlough. Again a star departed from the sky on her last journey. This time I made a wish. I prayed I'd reach Tel Aviv safely. I hadn't seen Sara for six months. She was still serving in the army too.

"Avigdor, are you asleep?" I asked, trying to loosen the straps of my backpack.

"No, no, I am not asleep, I am just thinking. I really don't believe we will ever leave this damned place," he said angrily. "The crossing next to the Negbah police station bothers me," Avigdor added. Negbah fortress was a former British police station now in Egyptian hands. The station was near Kibbutz Negbah, still under siege.

"Don't worry about this," I remarked. "The Egyptians don't patrol at night." Avigdor didn't answer.

"Attention, get ready, we are leaving." The order was given by Yoske, the company commandant. We stood up at once, correcting our backpacks, moving our rifles to our right hands.

"*Kadima* (forward)." We began to march cautiously. The contours of the shrubs and trees resembled human silhouettes. The danger of an unexpected ambush pumped adrenaline into our blood. Marching during the night was always easy in the absence of the murderous desert sun, besides which we were carrying light equipment. I looked at my wrist watch, thirty-five minutes had passed since we left the base, and it seemed like we were already hours on our way. On the horizon the Negbah fortress loomed ominously. From this strategic position the Egyptians would pour murderous artillery fire on the Kibbutz Negbah defenders.

"Sssshhh." The entire unit went down, not a word was spoken. An Egyptian patrol was several yards away. The voices in Arabic were audible. Slowly the patrol disappeared in the darkness.

We began to march again, relieved to have Negbah behind us. We were almost running, hearts pounding, blood rushing to our heads. After a short distance the asphalt road glimmered in the moon light. The trucks stood nearby, lights dimmed, drivers waiting, ready to move. The reconnaissance unit was waiting too, the very best of Palmach, the *Chayot Hanegev* (animals of the Negev). They knew every path, every hill, with no compass—only the stars to guide them.

"Move, quickly!"

One by one, we got into the trucks. The drivers started the engines. Everyone was down on the floors of the trucks. A whispered count before the departure.

"Okay, go."

"Thank God," Avigdor said relieved, "I thought this moment would never come."

The narrow road knifed through the fields. The moist scent of fresh opened earth penetrated our nostrils. Not too long before I had plowed the rocky slopes of Kibbutz Eilon. It was a short spell of happiness after Buchenwald. In the kibbutz I rediscovered the beauty of nature. Green slopes, orchards, vineyards, and above my head the brilliant blue sky. The grapes and the apples, chilled in the morning hours by the mountain dew. Sara had been reluctant to leave the kibbutz. She liked the peaceful course of life, so different from the turbulent life in the cities.

At dawn the convoy arrived in Tel Aviv. The army camp was located at the northern edge of the city, at Zabotinsky Street.

Benjamin, at left, serving in the Palmach at
a southern Negev camp, Israel, 1948.

Avigdor and I took showers, changed our shirts, slacks, socks, ready for the divine moment to leave. Many of the soldiers serving in the unit came from kibbutzim, moshavim, villages and towns, a people's army. We formed columns outside the barracks. The white blue flag on the tall mast was unfurled, fluttering in the morning sea breeze.

"Who is this guy next to Yoske?" I asked turning to Avigdor.

"I have no idea, I've never seen him before," Avigdor answered, somewhat perturbed.

"Attention soldiers," shouted the commanding officer. It was Colonel Nathan, in his thirties, medium height, blond, blue eyes. He stepped forward, staring at us. "Soldiers of the Ninth

Battalion," he began, "I have to make an important announcement. At dusk a ship arrived on the shore at Tel Aviv. The name of the ship is *Altalena*. The ship is loaded with arms for Etzel (*Irgun Zwai Leumi*, Menachem Begin's right wing militia). We have information that Begin himself is on the ship. An ultimatum has been given to the captain of the ship to hand over the arms to the Israeli Defense Forces. The ultimatum was flatly rejected. Preparations are underway to storm the ship. You will take part in this attack," Nathan concluded.

The silence was depressing. No questions of any kind. I couldn't believe it. The unexpected danger of fratricide was obvious, brother against brother, Holocaust survivor against Holocaust survivor. A new-born country already torn by different political views and greed for power. Colonel Nathan left. Yoske took command.

"I am sorry boys," he said with regret, "But we are faced with a coup d'etat. It looks like Begin wants to take over. I am ready to answer your questions," Yoske added.

"I cannot go," Dov Blozowski said, stepping out of the column.

"Why not?" Yoske asked bluntly.

"My brother is on the ship," Dov said, "We are Holocaust survivors."

Yoske's face went pale. He was facing an unusual situation, but he quickly regained his composure. "Dov, I am really sorry, we are in a state of war, the orders must be obeyed."

"What do you want me to do?" Dov said pleading.

"You will have to obey the order."

"How can I shoot at the ship knowing that my only brother is there?"

Yoske was adamant, not willing to compromise. Dov bit his lips, fighting back tears. Three years before he had survived Auschwitz with his brother. They had seen their parents walk into the gas chambers, and now another curse: kill your brother because he is a member of Etzel. Dov was a member of Mapam, the left wing militia.

"You don't give me any choice," Dov said trembling. "I am not going, you can kill me as well. The well-being of my country is important to me but not to the point where I have to hurt my brother. I am afraid to go because I might shoot the commanding officer who gives me the order to shoot," Dov concluded, stepping back. The moment he mentioned his brother, Berek came to my mind.

Yoske didn't answer. "All those who refuse to go, step out," Yoske ordered angrily. Without another thought I stepped forward. Avigdor also joined Dov, who already stood outside the columns. "All those who refuse the order are under arrest, hand your arms to the platoon commander," Yoske ordered. Humiliated in front of the whole company, we were led by the MP to the detention barrack.

Dov was mad. "How can they be so cruel. I was the only one who made this request, they could exclude me from this dirty job. I have a brother. We have different political views. I don't expect morality in war, but I am fighting Arabs, not Jews. To hell with politics! I don't intend to be prime minister. You know I will be glad to go to jail, this will be their loss, they will have to look for a machine gunner. The one who gives orders should know that the one who receives the orders has to use his own moral judgement. I will not take this from anyone. I love my country, but I am not fighting a war against my brother," Dov concluded.

The air in the barrack was stuffy, the scorching heat unbearable, flies all over.

"Here goes our beautiful furlough and my clean shirt. I waited six months to get to Tel Aviv," Avigdor said bitterly.

"Avigdor, don't complain, it was our choice to obey the order or not," I said firmly.

"At least they should have asked for volunteers," Avigdor remarked.

"Don't be foolish, no one would volunteer for this kind of a job," I said sadly.

After an hour of torturous waiting, an armed MP entered the room. The MP's never smelled of gun powder, always stupidly aloof in their spotless uniforms. "Follow me," the MP said dryly.

We were led to an adjacent barrack occupied by the high command. We entered a spacious room. Three colonels were sitting along an oblong table. On the table was an electric fan. Behind them, on the wall, were portraits of the founding fathers of the State of Israel, Theodore Hertzel and David Ben-Gurion. We stood attentively, our hands folded behind our backs, staring at the military judges. Nathan sat in the center of the table, studying some papers.

"The three of you," he began without lifting his eyes from the papers, "have excellent records. The most serious charges are against Dov Blozowski, a threat to kill a commanding officer. The lesser charges are against Avigdor and Benjamin, but still a serious offense of collaboration in such a threat. What do you have to say?" Colonel Nathan said, directing his question to Dov.

"I stated it explicitly before, maybe too loudly, but I was angry. My brother is on the ship. We are both Holocaust survivors. I should be excused from such a mission. I am sorry but I would rather go to jail. This order is against my moral principals," Dov concluded.

"Benjamin, why are you supporting this act of mutiny?" Nathan asked in a low voice.

I stared straight into Nathan's eyes. "There are striking similarities between our pasts. I volunteered to serve in Palmach. My brother was murdered by the Nazis. I am fighting against the Arabs, and I am not interested in killing my Jewish brothers. I got this well deserved furlough after six months. My wife is waiting for me. Please let me go. I am a soldier, not a politician," I concluded firmly.

The judges were whispering together. Then turning to Avigdor, Nathan asked, "What are your moral reasons for disobedience?"

"I am a *Sabra*, I have my parents, my brothers, my sisters. What more can I say. The men on the ship are my friends, we fought together in many battles. I just couldn't do it. They would never forgive me. They are bereft of love, parents. I am very fortunate for what I have. I am sorry for them. My defiance is a small contribution I can make in their support. I hope I've done the right thing and I am fully responsible for my actions," Avigdor concluded.

A fresh hot breeze penetrated through the open window, bringing the fragrance of flowers. The judges spoke in low voices among themselves.

"I have a verdict," Nathan said, visibly moved by the moral aspects of the case. "It will be unjust," he began, "to disregard what was said in this room. You are a part of the unfolding history. We heard your views, moral and humane, but the flagrant act of mutiny remains unchanged. We are at war. None of you can decide the validity of any given order, as cruel as it might be. Your act is an act of defiance, not justified on the basis of moral considerations. Obedience is the morality of the people's army, and we are the people's army," Nathan concluded. "Dov Blozowski, you are sentenced to two years in jail. Avigdor and Benjamin, your furloughs are cancelled. You will be sent immediately to the front line. Dismissed."

We left the room, escorted by the MP, our hearts broken. The verdict was humiliating, but there was a feeling of pride. If we had to do it again, we wouldn't do it differently.

"Do you know Avigdor," I said bitterly, "I don't care. I learned my lesson, no more blind obedience. A soldier is not a machine. I know bitterly the meaning of blind obedience. I am not making any comparison, but for a Jew to kill a Jew…this is much too much. I am glad about what I did, no regrets, no sleepless nights, no conscience pangs. I don't give a damn for this lost furlough. If I stay alive I have a good chance for another one. I owe a lot to Dov. He inspired me to be myself. I had a brother too," I concluded.

"Well, it's still sad," Avigdor said in anguish. "I think Menachem Begin was pushing for a showdown; in his wildest dreams he never anticipated that the ship would be stormed. He just grossly miscalculated, Ben-Gurion was firm. You don't tease a lion."

"You know, I never looked at it that way." I said, immersed in thoughts.

A few hours after the verdict, Avigdor and I were on our way back to the front lines in the Negev. Dov went to jail. The ship had been initially anchored in the vicinity of Kfar Vitkin. After the ultimatum was given, the ship left to go back to sea. The moment the ultimatum was rejected, the ship was hit by cannon fire, set aflame and scuttled on the shores of Tel Aviv. In the ensuing battle fourteen members of Etzel were killed, one member of Palmach died and a dozen more were wounded. It was the first time in modern Jewish history that Jewish blood was shed by Jews out of political differences and aspirations. On the ship were non-Jews, volunteers to fight the cause of the new-born state. Their shock was understandable.

Dov was set free after three months, never to return to his unit. The tragic debacle of the *Altalena* augured the demise of Etzel as well as the Palmach. Ben-Gurion didn't want private armies, from the right or from the left. Ben-Gurion wanted a strong IDF. The ship lay aground for months like a ghostly phantom, a sore wound on the Israeli conscience. Finally she was dragged away and sunk. In this irrational fratricidal flare-up there were strong undercurrents tinted by political aspirations. Many of the Palmach members who obeyed the order to storm the ship were Holocaust survivors. The patriotic tidings engulfing the *Altalena* were undisputable, but it narrowed down to killing, Jews against Jews. This was unacceptable. The people of Israel were aghast. *Altalena* was a flagrant case of mutiny endangering the very foundation of Israel democracy. Palmach had leftist tendencies. Etzel had rightist tendencies. But their devotion and loyalty to the cause of Israel was indisputable. The elimination of Etzel and Palmach opened a road to a strong and unified IDF. The *Altalena* was the eye of the storm.

We few who refused to shoot were guided by our moral compasses. Three years after my liberation from Buchenwald I regained the self esteem distorted by war's bestiality. I learned to function as an individual and decided once and for all not to be a pawn in the hands of order givers. The darkness of a human soul gave way to a brilliant brightness. The rushing stream of history doesn't stop at the pebbles or even the rocks.

18

EPILOGUE

THE PHONE call came from out of the blue. It was 1988 and we had been living quietly in Brooklyn, New York, for twenty-six years. We had just retired and were planning to move to Florida. Our two Israeli-born children, Avi and Ayelet, were grown and living on their own—Avi with his wife and two children near Washington, D.C., and Ayelet with her fiancé in Manhattan. The fortieth anniversary of the liberation of Buchenwald had come and gone with little notice, though an article in *The New York Times* did appear and included some inaccuracies that I wrote to correct. My letter to the editor was published a few days afterwards.

The caller had read the letter and had found me in the phone book. He said he was a television producer with the public television station in New York, and he was preparing a documentary about black American soldiers in Europe during World War II. He was interested in my letter's description of the American soldiers I remembered seeing on the day of my liberation: tall black men, the first I had ever seen in my life.

Reading about and remembering Buchenwald had churned up painful feelings, and I had been sleeping poorly, often waking with nightmares. I reluctantly agreed to meet him for an interview at his office in Manhattan later that week. I put the phone down and told Sara.

Sara looked at me and softly reassured me that this was the right decision. "Benjamin, we should close this Holocaust chapter once and for all, don't you think?"

A few days later I took the bus to Manhattan and arrived with plenty of time before the interview. I was quite nervous and some confusion at the reception desk with uniformed guards standing around did little to relax me. Fortunately I was soon led inside by an attractive woman, around forty, who turned out to be one of the producers, Nina Rosenblum. Her partner, Bill Miles, the man who had called me, was a sixtyish black man of medium height who had a warm smile. They made me feel comfortable and I sat down with them in their crowded office filled with awards and striking photographs.

They began to interview me using a small tape recorder. I described in detail the events of April 11, 1945. Nina led me through my memories with quiet questions, sometimes with just her eyes. It was difficult and soon both Nina and I were in tears. I felt tremendous relief when the interview ended and we all embraced warmly as I left.

The bus ride home was smooth and traffic was light. I arrived home in a good mood. Sara greeted me at the door.

"Benjamin, take a shower. Coming from the city is like going through a chimney. Dinner is ready and you haven't eaten all day. When you're tense you don't eat; when I am tense, I eat!"

I came down refreshed and during the meal Sara didn't ask any questions. She followed a simple rule: serve food first and ask questions later. She is an excellent cook. Finally we finished.

"So, how was it?"

"I think," I said, "I was able to deliver the right message about Buchenwald. The black soldiers that I saw the day of liberation never got any recognition, but I will always be grateful to them."

I slept well that night.

We were soon totally involved in the sale of our house and packing for the move to Florida. I went into the city for another audio interview but months passed and I didn't hear anything about the film. Finally, just as we were making the arrangements for the moving van, Nina called to ask me to appear for an on-camera interview.

They filmed a long conversation with me in a Manhattan studio the day before we left for Florida. I spoke of the years under German occupation, of the camps, of the loss, and of the liberation. It was very draining, but at the end there were embraces and tears, and I felt a chapter was ending.

We drove to Florida the very next day and began a new life. For us Florida was everything we had hoped for: a pace of life flowing like a quiet river, casual, affordable, practical. It required a little adjustment from Brooklyn. I got back into photography and writing, and we started going to the ballet and concerts—things we rarely did in New York. A fixed income goes a lot further in Florida.

Many months passed. Then a phone call from my daughter Ayelet in New York brought me back to the world we had left behind.

We speak in Hebrew with each other. "Abba, I just spoke with Nina. They've raised the money to finish the film and they're planning to go to Germany to film some sequences on location." She paused. "They want to film you in Buchenwald.

It might be hard for you, and you always told us you would never go back to Germany. It's up to you." She sounded concerned yet excited.

I was quiet for a moment and then I found myself telling her, "I understand, but I think it's important that I go. I cannot say no. This film is important. Am I right?"

"Yes, Abba, of course. I just hope it won't be too much for you. Make sure Emma is with you for support."

Ayelet and her fiancé, also a filmmaker, had become close friends of Nina and her husband Danny, and Nina had called them first to test the idea of a return to Buchenwald. Nina's call came in right after.

"Ben, this is Nina. I know I haven't been in touch lately, but this project is totally consuming and just keeps getting bigger. I hardly have time to breathe." She spoke calmly, though, and then lowering her voice she said, "Ben, are you ready for this one? We're going to Germany to film on site, we'll be in Berlin and Buchenwald." She paused and I was quiet. "Don't worry. Bill will be there too and you'll have good support. All the expenses will be covered."

I was silent. It was more real now and I froze for a moment. Finally I said, "Nina, Sara is standing right here. Would you like to say hello to her?"

Sara is very direct. She said, "Nina, I just heard about this trip to Buchenwald. I agree with you, Benjamin should go. He has to do it. It will help him come to terms with the past. I support the whole idea." She handed the phone back to me.

"Okay Nina, I am very anxious about the trip but we have a deal. I would like Sara to join me. I want her to see Weimar and Buchenwald. She will know a little more about my life. I know you have a tight budget so I will pay for her."

Nina said, "Thank you, Ben. We won't let you down. You will travel with two of the black veterans and our cameraman, Kevin. He's a great guy and you'll enjoy working with him. We'll meet in Berlin."

———

BERLIN...GERMANY...after forty-seven years I was to break a solemn vow never to set foot on German soil again. To walk again in hell surrounded by the ghosts of the past. It was unimaginable. I really believed in the importance of the film, though, and this kept up my resolve in the few days we had before the departure. Sara was a big comfort. She is very level headed.

We flew from Florida and were to rendezvous with our traveling companions at JFK Airport in New York. We had been sitting at the departure gate for a while when two black men in casual clothes finally came up to us and asked if we were the Benders. They didn't recognize the look of survivors in our healthy demeanors, and had been reluctant to approach us. They had memories too. We introduced ourselves—they were Leonard "Smitty" Smith and E.G. McConnell—and were soon joined by the cinematographer, Kevin Keating. These were all warm, friendly men and we were comfortable immediately. We arrived in Berlin without incident, although Kevin discovered an expensive lens missing when we collected our baggage. We spent the night at a hotel and in the morning we were joined by Klaus Hennig (the German co-producer), a still photographer and his assistant, additional film crew, and Nina and Bill. We loaded a van and two cars and set off for Buchenwald.

It was the end of June but the weather was cold and nasty, not a ray of sunshine. A chilly wind was howling off Hartz Mountain, a macabre sound that hadn't changed. Buchenwald was always cold. The vehicles stopped a few yards from the gatehouse. The iron gate with the inscription *Jedem das seine* looked smaller than I remembered it. I got out. Except for a few tourists walking briskly, it was deserted and surrounded by an eerie stillness. Time came to a standstill.

I approached the gate from what had been the German colony. I pressed down the handle on the gate and entered the roll call area. The barking of the SS guards was missing and nothing was left except two observation posts, barbed wire fences and some odd buildings, but no barracks. Beyond the roll call area I saw a cluster of buildings including the notorious Ward 46, where experiments on inmates were performed without anaesthesia, and the chimney of the crematorium. I closed my eyes and felt my heart pounding.

I recalled the snowy days when we had stood here for hours, frozen numb, waiting to be counted, inmates dropping dead one by one and no one paying any attention, the snow covering the bodies like a shroud. I opened my eyes and looked at the ground now covered with pebbles and black soil. Human ashes had been spread all over the camp and the adjacent roads. I was walking on sacred human ashes. I suddenly felt a chill. My heart was really pounding now, pumping adrenaline, a feeling of fear, of terror, was gripping me. I wanted to run. I wanted to cry. I had never really cried in Buchenwald, the Germans didn't allow it. Tears were a sign of weakness and only the strong could survive. The weak had to perish.

I was totally drained. I lifted my head and briefly caught

Klaus' eye. He lowered his gaze. I felt a hand on my shoulder. It was Nina, wearing a scarf of Sara's on her head. We walked away from the gate in silence.

The filming began with a flurry of activity. Kevin was everywhere: the rail line leading to Weimar, Ward 46, Building 50, the museum where human skin lampshades, heads, and body parts are still on display, the stump of the oak tree loved by Goethe, the observation posts, the barbed wire—nothing was left untouched. I led the crew to the execution room where I had counted 48 butcher hooks on the walls when I first saw the room after liberation; there were few left now. I described seeing broken fingernails on the floor and scratches on the walls where the victims had hung dangling in the air.

We reentered the gate with the camera rolling, me in the middle flanked by Smitty and E.G. on either side. I explained the inscription and we began to walk slowly while Kevin and Nina followed. I described the day of liberation and I turned to look at E.G. He's a little older than me, about five-nine, his dark hair topped with silver, with sensitive green eyes. He was searching for words, and was unable to come to terms with the evil that had ruled the Buchenwald inferno. Smitty was taller and heavyset, and his eyes emanated friendliness. As we got to the crematorium he embraced me and was unable to control his tears. He asked me, almost pleading, "Ben, Ben, how did you survive this?"

E.G. was visibly angry, his eyes gleaming with ire. He tried to control his turbulent thoughts. Finally he said, "Ben, tell me, what was your wish when you were finally liberated?"

I was caught by surprise. No one had ever asked me this before.

"So, Ben, did you have a desire for something special?"

"Yes," I said. "My wish wasn't new to me. It had been in my mind for years. Under the German occupation, even before Buchenwald, I was always hungry, yearning for bread. So my first wish was to get ahold of a large, crusty loaf of bread. I didn't want to slice it, but to tear it apart and stuff it in my mouth for maximum pleasure. I wanted to eat the bread all alone, in seclusion, like a dog working on his bone. I wanted to be away from the crowds. This wasn't just my dream. My brother had this dream too, but it never came true." I paused, thinking of my brother. I am still haunted by his memory.

"But I really had two wishes, not just one," I said finally. "My second wish was simple: to roll in the mud like a child."

I suddenly felt very old. I couldn't understand why this piercing pain was still with me. I was a slave of my memories, I now knew. I left the gate alone with my head bowed. I had one more task to perform. I walked slowly to the monument at the now barren site of the barracks. I had brought a few flowers with me and now I drew them from my jacket pocket. I held them together for a moment and placed them at the base of the monument, the only marker for the life I mourned most, my brother Berek. I was crying.

—

SARA HAD stayed out of camera range, sitting outside talking with Klaus. She had gotten nauseous in the crematorium when we first went in and decided not to continue the tour with us. She was also angry that there had been no mention of Jews in the memorial plaque, just "Poles." She was very direct with Klaus.

"You know Klaus, when I look at a German in his seventies I get nervous. I wonder about his background, simple as that." Klaus was silent. "Weimar is such a beautiful city with lots of proud German history. But I can't understand one thing: how could Buchenwald be so close to Weimar? Such culture so close to so much hatred and insanity." She was visibly angry now.

Klaus was probably forty-five. His dark blond hair was streaked with grey and he wore heavy rimmed glasses that accentuated his narrow eyes. He was reserved and rarely smiled, a bit aloof, but he knew a little Yiddish. His company, WDR, German public television, was coproducing the film with the New York station that Nina and Bill worked with. He was listening attentively but didn't say anything.

Sara continued, "Benjamin told me that the people he encountered in Weimar after his liberation claimed they didn't know, *Wir haben nicht gewusst*. Can you believe that? I mean there were slave markets in Weimar every day where the *Musulmans* of Buchenwald would be brought for work assignments. Right in the middle of Weimar."

"You've made your point Sara." Klaus said solemnly. "Weimar people undoubtedly knew all about this. Many of them were working in Buchenwald, doing business with the SS administrators."

They went back to the hotel to wait for us. The historic Elephant Hotel was located adjacent to the marketplace. On one side was the Rathaus with its huge roman clock on the top. Next door was the basement restaurant where we were to meet for dinner. The next building was the eighteenth century home of the Bach family. When I came in Sara and Klaus were in the lobby.

Klaus gave me a friendly wave. "Hello Ben. Where have you been?"

"I was exploring the streets of Weimar, trying to retrace my footsteps," I said lightheartedly.

"Did you find some?" He was looking directly at me, with some interest.

"Not really," I said. "I was looking for some of the beautiful public gardens I remember. They're now being restored, like the whole of Weimar. It's visible everywhere."

"Do you have a reason to look for the gardens?"

"Well," I said, haltingly, "yes. A lot of painful memories. In one of these gardens is a monument to Goethe, a great son of a different Germany. I didn't find it, but in Buchenwald I saw something depressing. There is a stone marker next to Ward 46 with Goethe's name engraved on it. Why there? For God's sake, this is an insult to Goethe's memory."

Sara interrupted. "I'm leaving you to continue this conversation. I've had enough. Really, it's too much, even now after forty-seven years. I'll see you later."

I continued, more quietly. "I admire and revere him. He was a humanitarian, he wrote about *Weltschmertz*, the pain of humanity. I really wanted to find his monument. I think there is a mausoleum in one of these gardens where he is buried next to his friend Johann Christoph Friedrich Schiller. Schiller was younger than Goethe and I think it was his wish to be buried next to his friend."

Klaus spoke carefully, "Ben, as far as I know, they are not buried in the same place."

I paused, a little embarrassed. "My memory may be off..."

Bill and Nina came in, exhausted but elated. They were very

pleased with the filming. Kevin was doing an excellent job and their years of preparation were bearing fruit. Nina in particular was emotionally drained. She is Jewish, and her father, a well-known photographer, had been with U.S. forces in the first days of liberation and got the first photographs of Dachau. She was trying to create an extraordinary documentary, covering not just the participation of black soldiers in the liberation of some of the concentration camps, but also weighing on her mind were those who died in Buchenwald, and those who were lucky to survive.

"You know Ben, you did very well," she said. I was pleased. The long, hard day had been worth it.

The next day Klaus came up to me smiling, almost giggling. He said, "Ben, I apologize, you were right. Goethe was buried next to Schiller, right here in Weimar. I regret I didn't know the facts."

"I'm glad you told me," I said. "I was beginning to think my mind was going. You know, Klaus, there is another figure I like in German literature, a poet and lyricist. His books were destroyed by Hitler even before *Krystallnacht*. He wrote *Lorelei*. His name was Heinrich Heine. '*Dort oben am Gipfel des Berges…*(There, above the mountain peak…)' He wrote about a beautiful nymph with golden hair. He was a converted Jew, too."

"Yes, I know, but you missed a line. It starts like this: '*Was soll das bedeuten…*(What does it mean…).'"

"Klaus, you're absolutely right," I said, smiling. "Now we're even." I looked around. "You know, I love this Hotel Elephant. I didn't realize it but I discovered today that the market just outside was the place we used to come to be picked for work, what we called the slave market. Right here, with the Bach house next door. Amazing."

Klaus became thoughtful. He said, "Ben, would you mind if I ask you a personal question? Perhaps I shouldn't, it's a sensitive issue…"

"No, go ahead," I said, "I don't mind."

"Do you still hate the German people for what you experienced during the war, especially in Buchenwald?"

I didn't answer right away. I was trying to find the words. Finally I said, "The entire German nation is not blameless for the mass murder of innocent people. Too many Germans from all walks of life were active accomplices in this crime. I am the last of a family of twenty-five—parents, brother, grandparents, uncles, aunts, cousins and more. These innocent people were killed for being Jews. The mother of hatred is ignorance, but how can you hate without knowing someone? But this is exactly what the Nazis did. They taught how to hate, even schoolchildren. Human beings, healthy and talented, were considered vermin, outcasts, *Untermensch*. I can't hate, but I despise the blind and stupid German obedience to orders to kill. This insanity is beyond my comprehension."

Klaus was silent and his face was pale, his eyes twinkling. "Ben," he said at last, "I am ashamed. I shouldn't have asked this question. As a German of the post-war generation I have no answer, no explanation for the crimes committed by our parents. I can't even ask them questions, I'd just get standard answers…"

"Klaus," I said, "you visited the museum. Did you see the giant memorial plaque where they have the list of nationalities? Did you see any mention of Jews or Gypsies who died in Buchenwald? This is another betrayal of human memory."

"I understand your point, but perhaps Jews were classified according to their country of origin. After all, Jews were living in many countries…"

"Okay, I know what you're trying to say," I said, "so let's assume for a moment that Jews were considered Polish or French or whatever. Please listen carefully. During my last days in the camp I was in the hospital and the loudspeaker from the gatehouse was blasting instructions about the evacuation of the small camp. I heard the following repeatedly: '*Achtung, Achtung, samtliche Juden ans Tor!*' Do you follow me? These commands were given to thirty thousand Jews, not to the Poles, Hungarians, British, or French."

Klaus spoke with some uneasiness. "Ben, you're right. There is a tendency to cover up the truth here. I wish I knew why. The East German communists did a nice job. They've erected memorials for their own purposes. I really hope this film will help tell the truth."

"I hope so too. It might be too late," I said, a little upset.

"You've had a heck of a life…"

"I wasn't a hero. I did nothing to steer events, I was just at the mercy of fate, nothing more. What really bothers me are the missing chapters of my life—school, childhood, parents, girls, normal life. The wounds will never heal."

Klaus was immersed in thought and didn't show any emotion. Perhaps he had heard these stories many times. He said, "What do you think of today's Germany, after the unification?"

"Well, I think it was inevitable. It was just a matter of time. The same culture, the same language, discipline, diligence. This time I would exclude the word obedience. Germans are hard working people. They may have learned the hard way, tempered by the past."

"Do you see any danger in reunification?"

"No, not at all. Communism is dead. There is enough *Lebensraum* for everybody. Germany has to live on a par with other nations, no more superiority complex. Open borders, open minds, and a willingness to help other countries in need. Germany is Europe, and the day is near when we may have a United States of Europe. No more *Eintritt Verboten.*"

The elevator opened and Sara got off and headed our way. "Oh boy, you're back where I left you yesterday." She was smiling. "Have you solved the urgent global problems?"

"I took your husband's time but we had a very interesting exchange of views," Klaus said. He put his hand in his pocket and took out a *pfennig* and, handing it to her, said, "Sara, I have a little *Andenkung* for you. According to German tradition, this will be a good omen. You might get rich."

"Thank you, Klaus, let me reciprocate," she said smiling. She took out her wallet and gave him a quarter, a dime, and a nickel. Klaus was elated, and then, to his astonishment, Sara embraced him warmly.

—

WE LEFT the next morning. The film crew went on to Dachau. We took the train to Berlin and then a taxi to the airport. We were leaving Germany with a sense of relief. Even with all the German hospitality we were anxious to get home as soon as possible. Berlin, Weimar, Buchenwald—this was behind us now.

ACKNOWLEDGMENTS

WORDS OF acknowledgment are a warm reminder of some of those who illuminated my life on the long and difficult path to publication of this book.

Nina Rosenblum and William Miles came out of the blue and included me in their Academy Award-nominated film *Liberators*. They are beautiful people in my life, and they gave me the confidence to continue. I am deeply grateful to them both, and to their colleagues on location in Berlin and Weimar: Kevin Keating, Simon Chaput, Anna Maryke, and Klaus J. Henning, and especially to Leonard (Smitty) Smith, whose friendship my wife and I continue to enjoy.

My deep gratitude goes to Elie Wiesel. We haven't met yet, but we've had a continuous exchange of warm letters for over twenty years. John P. Marquand, Jr. has been a friend and supporter for years, and he introduced me to William and Rose Styron who provided kind advice and encouragement. Martin Gilbert and Sir Brian Urquhart I thank for their warm notes and interest. Others who have written to me with support, suggestions, and advice include Arthur Kurzweil, Robert Loomis, and Claire Wachtell.

To Rabbi Meir Israel Lau, I am deeply appreciative of his blessings and kind words of encouragement. To my friend

Nedo Fiano, with whom I shared the torment and hopes of our day of liberation from Buchenwald, I say: the bonds between us were invisible then, but they did exist, and continue to this day. He and his wife Riri kindly recommended me to Daniel Vogelmann in Florence, who enthusiastically agreed to publish this book in Italy (for which I am very grateful), and who, in an amazing coincidence, turns out to be the nephew of the rabbi who officiated at my wedding in 1948!

My son Avi (with his wife Lili) was the first to show interest in my writings and helped prepare the first draft. This was the beginning. My daughter Ayelet and her husband Gaetano Maida helped shape this book into its final form. If not for their continuous support and effort, this work would not exist.

And most of all, my profound love and gratitude to my wife of nearly fifty years, my devoted companion, Sara.

ABOUT THE AUTHOR

BORN IN Czestochowa, Poland, Benjamin Bender survived the Buchenwald concentration camp and went on to become a veteran of Israel's War of Independence. He and his family emigrated to the United States in 1962. Since his appearance in the film *Liberators*, he has been speaking before groups about the Holocaust. Retired from business, he is a writer, painter, and photographer, and lives with his wife, Sara, in Boynton Beach, Florida.

The author at the Buchenwald concentration camp during the filming of Liberators, *1991.*